Know What I Mean?

Know What I Mean?

Frank Bruno

with Norman Giller

Stanley Paul

London, Melbourne, Auckland, Johannesburg

This book is dedicated to the memory
of Robert Bruno. My Dad. My hero.

Acknowledgements

Frank Bruno and Norman Giller would like to thank Roddy Bloomfield
and his gifted team at Stanley Paul for all their work in our corner.
Without their sterling efforts the following pages would be blank! In
particular we would like to thank picture researcher Gabrielle Allen for
her diligence, Marion Paull and Francesca Liversidge for their editing
skills, Bob Vickers for his design work, and Patrick McCreeth for fitting
us with a striking jacket. Special thanks also to photographers Monty
Fresco, Eamonn McCabe, Guglielmo Galvin, Tommy Hindley, Steve
Rapport, Lawrence Lustig and Chris Smith for their knockout pictures,
and also to the following sources for helping to keep us in the picture:
Daily Mail, Daily Express, The Star, The Sun, News of the World,
Sunday Mirror, The People, The Standard, Thames Television, BBC
Enterprises, LWT, All-Sport Photographic, Associated Press, Colorific!,
G. Cossey, Global Pictures, London Features International, Duncan Paul
Associates, Press Association, Sport & General, Sporting Pictures
(UK), Syndication International and Universal Pictorial.

Stanley Paul & Co. Ltd
An imprint of Century Hutchinson Ltd
Brookmount House, 62-65 Chandos Place,
Covent Garden, London WC2N 4NW

Century Hutchinson Group (Australia) Pty
16-22 Church Street, Hawthorn,
Melbourne, Victoria 3122

Century Hutchinson (NZ) Ltd
32-34 View Road, PO Box 40-086,
Glenfield, Auckland 10

Century Hutchinson (SA) (Pty) Ltd
PO Box 337, Bergvlei 2012, South Africa

© **Frank Bruno, Norman Giller 1986**

Set in 12pt Times

Printed and bound in Great Britain
by Butler & Tanner Limited, Frome, Somerset

ISBN 0 09 168540 0

Contents

Introduction: Seconds Out

Thanks for joining me in my corner. If I said I was *writing* this book I would be starting off with a lie, and that's no way to begin what I want to be an honest record of all that I have done on the way to a world title fight. With the sort of education I've had I'm no Frederick Forsyth. More of a Bruce! But then, could Frederick Forsyth challenge for the world heavyweight championship? I've *talked* the book and have told the story of being a hungry fighter to Norman Giller, a hungry writer, who has listened and got my words down in what I hope are the right order. He normally writes books with his old mate Jimmy Greaves, but I thought it would be nice for him to listen to a refined accent for a change!

This isn't my life story. I've got my best years still to come, please God, and will get between the covers with an autobiography when I'm much older and wiser. It's more of a scrapbook account of all that's happened to me so far. I shall be talking about the people I've met on the way up, the fights I've had and the troubles I've seen. There have been good times and bad times, and I look forward to sharing my memories with you. If nothing else, you'll find in the following pages that I've become an accomplished name-dropper. I have cuddled Bo Derek, clowned with Freddie Starr, Les Dawson and a dozen other great comics, spouted Shakespeare with Lenny Henry, been introduced to Prince Philip, gone to the races with Terry Wogan, picked the brains of Larry Holmes, sat at the feet of Muhammad Ali, been crushed by the Bonecrusher, have flown with George Michael, swapped stories with Telly Savalas, Tom Selleck, Burt Reynolds and Jack Nicholson, played snooker with Steve Davis, been sent up by 'Spitting Image' ('Fank you, 'Arry!') and have had the good fortune to be steered along the right path by Terry Lawless, a manager in a million. It's not been bad so far for a poor black Cockney kid from south of the Thames who was so bright at school that when he was asked by a teacher where the Magna Carta was signed he said: 'At the bottom of the page, Miss.'

It's Terry Lawless who is wise enough to tug on my arm every now and again and whisper: 'Don't forget where you've come from.' He has guided four boxers to world championships and knows that all the publicity and alleged fame can have a false foundation. And if that doesn't sound like me talking it's because I'm quoting Terry who is determined to keep my feet on the ground.

But there's no danger of me forgetting my roots. I've got mental scars to remind me how tough it was in the early days when I was heading down the wrong road to what could easily have been a life of crime. I recently had to fill in one of those 'Star File' forms sent to me by a magazine and one of the questions was: 'What would you have been if you hadn't been a boxer?' Just for a laugh I scribbled in 'A black Ronnie Biggs'.

Then I stopped and thought about it and realised that what I meant as a joke wasn't far from the truth. A lot of my old schoolmates and street rivals drifted into trouble and are now looking out at the world from behind bars. I could so easily have been in prison with them but for boxing.

It's the thought of what I might have been that keeps me on my toes, jabbing and moving. **Know what I mean?**

1: The First Punches

A lot of my fights you won't find in the record books and one in particular changed my life. It was against my schoolteacher. I was just eleven years old at the time and what you might call something of a handful, know what I mean?

To look at the pictures of me on these pages as an angelic, sweet-faced kid it's hard to imagine that I was a little tearaway. Correction - a *big* tearaway. I was always head and shoulders above other kids my age and I used to throw my weight around. Looking back, I now realise that all my aggression was just a way of expressing

Here I am at two - looking ready to terrorise the world's heavyweights!

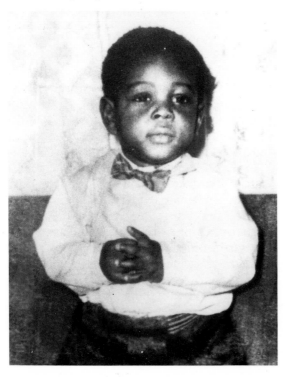

myself. I wasn't too clever at doing it with words, and so I used to get my message across in a physical way. I just wanted to be noticed, but in the eyes of most people in the South London streets of Wandsworth where I grew up I was a bully boy.

Lynette, my lovely Mum, had to deal with all the mums and dads who used to wear a path to our street door to complain about me. 'Look at what your Frank's done to my boy,' was the usual opening line. Then when they'd gone off, Mum would turn to me and say: 'Franklyn, just wait until your father gets home. What *are* we going to do with you. We need all the help the good Lord can give us to stop you becoming a sinner.'

Mum talks just like that. She preaches at the Pentecostal church and she has dedicated her life to the word of God. She is proud of what I have achieved, but finds it hard to accept the violence in my sport. Whenever I climb into the ring she stays at home praying that neither I nor my opponent gets hurt.

She was a district nurse in South London for many years and was well looked after when she went into Hammersmith Hospital to have me on November 16, 1961. I was nine pounds for my first weigh-in and mum says that because a lot of the hospital staff knew her they all made a fuss of me. "He's going to grow up to be somebody special," she told them. I hope I've made her words come true but it's not in quite the way she would have intended. Her choice of profession for me would have been a banker but in my early days it seemed more likely that I might grow up to become a bank robber.

I gave Mum a really hard time as a kid.

She tells me that even before I was a year old I used to smash my way out of my wooden cot and that I was always making a fist and thumping things. Mum and Dad had come over from the West Indies years before I was born and were among the first black families to move into Wandsworth. We lived in a rambling old terraced house in Barmouth Road where Mum still lives to this day surrounded by all her friends and memories of her full Christian life. I grew up there with my three sisters, Faye, Angela and Joanne and my big brother Michael. Another brother, Eddie, lives in Jamaica which is the sunshine island where Mum grew up. Michael stands a whopping six feet five inches and is twelve years older than me. He's always been my number one fan, and even before I turned pro he had written on the wall above our kitchen door: 'FRANK BRUNO, HEAVYWEIGHT CHAMPION OF THE WORLD 1986.'

I was the youngest of the Brunos, and according to Mum I gave her more trouble than the rest of them put together. The first day she took me to school at nearby Swaffield Primary I ran off the minute she walked out of the playground. She dragged me back the next day and from then on I was something of a rebel pupil. I had restless energy and hated sitting at a school desk for hours on end listening to teachers talking about things that just didn't interest me. I became a dreamer and used to sit with my thoughts wandering while the words of the teachers droned miles over my head. One moment I'd be seeing myself in my mind's eye as Gary Sobers, whacking sixes around the ground and taking wickets with every ball I bowled. Then I'd become a centre-forward like Peter Osgood who I used to love watching play for Chelsea at Stamford Bridge. I was about nine when my daydreams suddenly became taken up full-time with boxing. My imagination was captured by the magic of Muhammad Ali who was just starting a comeback in preparation for his 'Fight of the Century' against Smokin' Joe Frazier.

I'm taking a lap of honour with my mum and younger sister Joanne. I think Joanne's wondering what her little brother is going to get up to next

I was completely hooked on the legend of Ali. I used to try his moves out in the playground at Swaffield Primary School where I rarely floated like a butterfly but managed to sting like a bee. 'Bruno, report to the headmaster,' became a common instruction as I landed punches on kids who were reluctant opponents. I was told the place to use my fists was in a proper boxing club and so I joined the Wandsworth Boys Club where I put gloves on for the first time. I can remember it so well that it hurts.

One of the trainers, a Mr Levington, had heard about my reputation for being a bully and decided I needed putting in my place. He looked around for a boy to spar with me and selected his son, Gary, who was at least five years older than me but the only one about my size. It turned out that Gary was not only an experienced amateur boxer but also a southpaw, which meant he led with his right fist and right foot forward. Now in all my daydreaming of being the next Muhammad Ali it had never entered my head that you met 'wrong way round'

9

My two sisters Angela and Joanne are as pretty as a picture, but I think my thoughts are on what my school pals would say if they could see me now. It's hardly a tough-guy image!

walking his beat. He's Gary Levington who has made a successful career for himself with the old Bill and has regularly won the Open Police Boxing Championship.

The only problem I had as a member of the Wandsworth Boys' Club boxing squad was that there was nobody around at my weight in my age group. I had three contests - all against the same opponent, a big, strong white boy called Gary Hill. I won two and he won one. In my first year at the club I became National Association of Boys' Clubs champion, but it was a bit of an empty triumph because I got a bye in every round including the final! They just couldn't find anybody big enough to match against me.

The silliest fight I ever had led to me leaving not only the Wandsworth Boys Club, but also my school and - this was the hardest part - I had to leave home as well. There was a particular master at my school who had taken an instant dislike to me. The feeling was mutual. I reckoned he was a flash, arrogant so-and-so and he reckoned I was a bully who needed putting in my place. We were probably both right in our assessments. It all blew up between us one afternoon when we were out for a sports lesson in a park near the Houses of Parliament. One of the girls from my class had a camera that I wanted to borrow. I think I might have forgotten to say please. Anyhow there was suddenly a tug of war for the camera between the teacher and me. The next thing I knew the camera was on the floor and he and I were wrestling with each other. I would describe it as more a scuffle than a fight, but the teacher had no doubts that I was trying to whack him one. Perhaps he was right, but I held myself back and pushed him around a bit. All I know is that I suddenly realised the stupidity of what I was doing and let go of him and ran off as fast as my legs would carry me. 'You're in real trouble this time, Bruno,' he shouted after me. I was scared out of my life because I knew I'd gone too far.

opponents. I just didn't know how to handle him and he gave me a mummy and a daddy of a hiding. His right jab hit me so many times on the nose that just thinking of it makes my eyes water.

I'm sure Mr Levington didn't expect to ever see me again, but I'd got the bug and was back there the next night and became a regular at the training sessions. I sometimes get a reminder of that first experience with the gloves on when I'm driving through London and spot a certain policeman

Relatively speaking, the support of my family means a lot to me. My backing group here are my big brother Michael and sisters Faye, Angela and Joanne. Another brother, Eddie, lives in Jamaica

I begged my Mum not to make me go to school the next day, but she dragged me there and into the headmaster's study. He shook his head gravely and looked down at a written report that the teacher had given him. 'It seems all the warnings I've given you in the past have not worked,' he said. 'I can't have pupils going around hitting members of my staff. I have no alternative but to expel you.'

As I tearfully left his study I know it didn't enter either of our heads that I would one day be invited back as guest of honour to present the school prizes.

Mum hardly said a word to me on the way home. She had heard of a school that catered for difficult boys and her mind was ticking over as to how she could get me there. A couple of days later she told me: 'Franklyn, I've got you a place at Oak Hall Boarding School. You start there next next week.'

Boarding school? I didn't even know what a boarding school was. When I realised it meant I had to leave home to go there I cried my eyes out. I begged my Mum to change her mind but she said firmly: 'Franklyn, it's for your own good. You need saving from the devil that's inside you.'

2: School for Scoundrels

When people talk about boarding schools they automatically think of places like Harrow and Eton. Oak Hall wasn't quite in that league. To be honest, it was a school for young scoundrels who needed straightening out. It was funded by the Greater London Council, and the one subject in which everybody was expected to get an honours degree was *discipline*.

At first I hated my Mum for sending me there. I found it impossible to believe that she could be so cold hearted. But now I can see she did it for all the right reasons. I was running wild and needed the kick up the behind that the school gave me. Infact I can now look back and say that going to the school was one of the best things that ever happened to me.

But on my first day there I wondered what the hell Mum had let me in for. The all-boys school is in the middle of the Sussex countryside and could have been a million miles from the back streets of Wandsworth. When I was told I would be sleeping in a dormitory I thought they meant in the back of a van. How was I to know the difference between a dormitory and a Dormobile? The dormitory and dining room were in an old Victorian English country house that I now know to be beautiful, but which at first glance looked to my young eyes like a haunted house. The actual school building was a half-mile walk away down a leafy country lane past a home for old ladies. I bet there would have been a few nightmares in there if they had known that every day about fifty of London's roughest, toughest problem kids were walking by to and from the school house.

Not that any of us would have dared step out of line. The schoolteachers had been handpicked for their ability to cope with hard cases. A couple of them would have made ideal prison warders, and could have broken any of us in two if we had tried the sort of jack-the-lad stuff that had got me into so much bother at dear old Swaffield Primary.

Within a few hours of checking in at the school I was taken on one side by one of about half a dozen other black kids among the pupils. He was three years older than me, but we were about the same size. 'Right, Bruno, get it into your head right now that I run things here,' he said with real menace in his voice. 'You do things the way I tell you and you'll be all right. If you don't you'll have me to answer to. Okay me son?' He was a black Cockney from Eltham called Gunther Roomes. Little did we know it then that a few years later we would both be professional boxers in the Terry Lawless stable. At first I was frightened stiff of Gunther but we learnt to respect each other and became pals.

On my first five or six nights at the school I cried myself to sleep. Why had Mum done this to me? If I run away how can I get home? Will Gunther and his mates beat me up tomorrow? I tried running away but was caught by a teacher who gently talked me into returning. 'It's for your own good,' she told me. 'Give it a chance and I promise you that you will enjoy your stay at Oak Hall.' By the time the second week came around I was beginning to settle to the school routine and within a month I was hardly giving a thought to Wandsworth. They didn't try so much to exercise the mind at Oak Hall as the body. Most of what

The Oak Hall cricket team. This picture was taken when I was thirteen and dreaming of becoming a combination of Michael Holding and Gary Sobers. But I now know that I would rather face the punches of Tim Witherspoon than the bouncers of Malcolm Marshall

we did was aimed at eating up our surplus energy. Every day there was action of some sort. Among the sports I tried and enjoyed were basketball, canoeing, horse riding, swimming, gymnastics, weightlifting, judo, tennis, athletics, cross country running and roller skating. My favourites were cricket in the summer and football in the winter. I used to bowl fast and imagined I was Michael Holding as I ran in, and I dreamt of one day playing for England. Just think, if I

had stuck at it I might have been sharing the new ball attack with Ian Botham. Mind you, then I might have been getting the stick from the media that he gets. I don't think it's fair the way he gets hounded. Everybody - sportsmen, show-business celebrities, pop stars and politicians - is entitled to keep his private life private.

I was still trying to be a Peter Osgood on the football field but had none of his silken skills. I was all aggression in the No. 9 shirt and was continually getting in trouble with the referees for going in too strong. I got picked for the Sussex Schools team, but I had doubts whether I could make it as a professional footballer. Already I was mapping out a future in my mind to become a professional boxer. I knew it was where the big money was, and even from about the age of thirteen I used to tell people who asked me my ambition: 'I want to become a multi-millionaire.'

The one sport not included on the Oak Hall agenda was boxing. It had been banned by the GLC, but there were a couple of sets of gloves in the gymnasium and whenever two boys started arguing they were sent to the gym to settle their differences with the gloves. I used to enjoy that and usually got the better of any of the boys that I fell out with. In fact my jab sickened so many of them that after a time nobody used to pick rows with me, know what I mean? I used to spend every spare second in the gym, working out with weights and following a general fitness programme that helped lay the foundation for the physique I have today.

The Class of '74. Me and my Oak Hall schoolmates on a day trip to Hastings. There was no Battle of Hastings that day. We were on our best behaviour because we knew we would lose all privileges if we put a foot out of place

The great thing about Oak Hall was that you were taught to be independent. We went on a lot of camping breaks where we had to do our own cooking, and while at school we had to make our own beds, clean our shoes every morning, keep the dormitory tidy, serve at the dinner tables and help out in the kitchen. You had to be respectful at all times and always stand up when a teacher walked into the room.

If you did break the strict school rules the punishment was quick and painful. The teachers were armed with slippers that they whacked you with until you were bruised and sore. In my first year I felt the full weight of the slipper a dozen times, but I gradually learned my lesson and I was as sweet as a pussycat by the time I was into my second year.

Some boys never learned and I saw them take terrible punishment, including getting thumped by teachers driven to taking desperate measures to maintain discipline. Several times boys used to run away, and when they were brought back they would find all their privileges withdrawn. They

I'm playing the waiting game here in my last day at Oak Hall. It was a tradition of the school that any boys who had done well during the last term served lunch on the final day. Oak Hall served me the best possible foundation for what I was about to do with the rest of my life. The pretty girl, by the way, is the headmaster's daughter

would not be allowed to go on the evening outings to Hastings or Eastbourne and would be detailed to work parties whose jobs included sweeping the long drive, picking up every loose leaf, scrubbing the floors and cleaning out the toilets. In a way I suppose it was like being in the Army, but I found I enjoyed the discipline and nowadays I take it for granted that I have got to get up off my behind and do things for myself.

It was while I was at Oak Hall that I converted to Roman Catholicism and - as with my Mum - religion has become an important foundation to my life. I don't preach to people about it, but find I get personal contentment in going to church regularly and having a commitment to God. When I say 'thank God' after fights I am not just using empty words. The Bible is the only book that I read. It goes with me wherever I go and I often quote it to myself when I want inner strength.

I was a real handful for the teachers at Oak Hall when I first arrived, but I amazed them and myself by settling so well that by my final year I was the head boy. I would like to go on record here and now with a word of thanks to Headmaster Allan Lawrence and his staff for all they did to shape me into a responsible young man.

Most of all I want to thank my Mum for having the good sense to send me there. But I wish I had been at home to help her cope with the crisis that hit my family when my dear Dad died.

3: My Dad, My Hero

The one regret I have about my boxing career is that my dad is not around to see what I have achieved. I desperately wanted him to be proud of me, but he died before I was able to prove I could make something of myself. And to this day I am haunted by my dad's death.

He had come over from Dominica, one of the Windward Isles, long before I was born to seek his fame and fortune. All he found really was a lot of broken promises. He never had the luck he deserved, and when I was about ten he became desperately ill with diabetes and was then struck down by a stroke that paralysed him down one side.

It put enormous pressure on my mum, who as a district nurse had her hands full coping with the problems of other people. This was another reason she sent me away to school. At least with me out of the way she could concentrate on looking after Dad and didn't have to spend her time sorting out the trouble that I was causing with my over-aggressive attitude.

I have lovely as well as painful memories of my dad, who I will always rate as my number one hero. He was a quiet, thoughtful, big-boned man who always talked good common sense. 'Franklyn,' he'd say to me, 'just do what your mother tells you and you won't go far wrong. God gave you hands to be constructive not destructive. Now be a good boy or I'm going to have to give you a hiding that will hurt me more than it hurts you.'

True to his word, Dad used to give me the occasional good hiding. He used to keep a curtain rod hidden in a cupboard and when I was getting out of hand he used to take it out and whack my behind with all the power of Gary Sobers hitting a six. I mention Sobers because he was one of Dad's idols and he used to spend hours listening to the radio Test commentaries and cheering on the West Indies. Even after his stroke had meant he was confined to bed he still used to find ways of giving me a whack with the rod. He would hide it under the bedclothes and then call me to his room.

'Come round this side of the bed, son,' he would say, making sure I couldn't bolt out of the door, and also so that I was on the side of his body that he could still move. Then he would suddenly produce the rod and give me a whack across the behind. 'Your mother deserves better from you, Franklyn,' he would say. 'Do as she says or you will be in big trouble.'

But despite the whacks (that I always deserved) I never once lost my love and respect for my dad, and it really grieved me to see him in such pain in his last few years. It became so hard for him to bear that when I used to be home on school holidays mum had to show me how to give him his injections. If she was out on a call and dad suddenly cried out with pain I had to go and get the needle and stick it as gently as I could into dad's arm. I promise you I have never had such a difficult thing to do in my life. To this day it has made me very squeamish about needles, and if I ever have to go to hospital for treatment I am not the greatest patient in the world.

I was into my last year but one at Oak Hall when my housemaster, Mr Nicholls, took me to one side and told me quietly: 'I'm sorry to have to tell you, Frank, that your father has become critically ill. We

My dad, my hero. He was a lovely, warm, gentle man who never had the luck that he deserved. My big regret is that he is not around to see the success I am having in the ring. I hope and pray that he is proud of me

have arranged for you to catch the next bus so that you can go home to him.'

An odd and frightening thing happened during the long bus journey back to London. I was sitting looking out of the window when I heard my father's voice in my head as clearly as if he was sitting next to me. He was crying and calling out my name. When I finally got home my Mum was sitting in an armchair weeping. 'I'm sorry, Franklyn,' she said, 'but the good Lord has taken your father. He died while you were on your way home. He is out of his pain now and in the arms of our Father.'

I went to my bedroom and broke down

17

and cried. My Dad always thought I was something special. He used to tell me that if I put my mind to it I could make a success of my life. My brother Michael repeated recently what my Dad once said: 'God's spotlight shines down and picks out certain people. You're one of the chosen ones.'

As I cried in my room I secretly vowed to do something that would make my Dad, up there in Heaven, proud of me. Really proud.

By the time I left school I had made up

This is me at seventeen soon after I had started my amateur career with the Sir Philip Game club. Even at this early stage I had made up my mind that I would one day fight as a professional

my mind that the only way I was going to make anything of myself was as a professional sportsman. My academic qualifications were, to be honest, pathetic. I was fair at adding up (I prefer to count money than spend it!), but reading and writing were hardly my strong points. These days I could kick myself for not paying more attention in class, and if there are any youngsters reading this book I beg them to learn from my mistakes and take full advantage of their education. You only get the one chance and must grab it while you can.

I don't like being portrayed as a thicko. 'Spitting Image' gives me a lot of stick ('Fanks, know what I mean Arry?') but I think I could teach their scriptwriters a thing or two about life and about how to survive in the mean streets after starting out with nothing. I know I can buy and sell a lot of people when it comes to street sense. But I have to own up and admit that if you're going to judge me by my knowledge of the stuff you learn from books I ain't exactly the Brain of Britain, know what I mean?

So when I left school I knew that sport offered me the only way out of what could so easily have become a life of crime. I considered football because in my last season I had banged in more than 100 goals, but I knew in my heart that I was too aggressive and would just keep getting in trouble with the referees. Then I thought about cricket but decided that the really big money wasn't there unless you made it right to the very top.So I said to myself: 'Frank, baby, it's gotta be boxing.'

I joined the Sir Philip Game Amateur Boxing Club in South London and started building the foundation for what I knew deep in my own mind was going to be a professional career. At the same time as training and boxing I was working eight hours a day as a metal polisher. Now that has got to be one of the worst jobs on earth. I used to slave away in a small room and the heat and smell was enough to knock over a horse. God knows what I used to get into my lungs, but there were times when I would stagger out of the room where I worked as if I had been whacked on the chin by, dare I say it, Bonecrusher Smith. Somehow I stood it for a year, and at £43 a week it was slave labour. I could easily have signed on the dole, but I have always wanted to be able to stand on my own two feet and be beholden to nobody.

Next I got a job helping out a plumber as a humper. It was my job to hump the heavy stuff. Have you ever tried getting a bath up six flights of stairs? I used to get more bruised and bloodied knuckles doing that than I've ever got in the ring. One of my favourite comedians is Norman Wisdom, and some of the things that happened to me when I was lugging the baths, toilets and cylinders around could have come right out of one of his films. I've been stuck on landings with a bath digging into my gut, have tripped over pipes and flooded rooms, and once carted a bath to the top of a terrace house only to find I was at the wrong address. A strong humper I may be. A plumber I ain't.

My third job was on a building site and that was the hardest graft I ever did. I was the 'boy' in the gang and had to do all the running about. If there were tools to be collected, it was Bruno who would get them. If there were slabs of concrete to be shifted, it was Bruno who would move them. If there were ladders to be carried, it was Bruno who carried them. If there were tea and sandwiches to be picked up from the cafe, it was Bruno who went and got them. The memory of all that has stayed with me, and whenever I'm finding the going tough in training I just think back to those hard days and how boxing has rescued me and given shape and meaning to my life.

I just hope the people who want to ban boxing read this. I know all the risks involved and that you can get badly hurt in the ring. But let's be honest, they could ban boxing tomorrow and I'd switch to, say, cricket and might get killed by a bouncer to the head. I thought that what the England

This is the woman whose strength of character I hope I have inherited - my mum, who is the cleanest living and most honest woman I know. She doesn't like the violence of boxing and prays that neither I nor my opponents get hurt

batsmen were facing in the West Indies during the tour of 1986 was far more dangerous than anything I've ever had to face in the ring. So after banning boxing, I suppose they'll then try to outlaw cricket. We'll finish up with only tiddlywinks and croquet as sports considered safe.

My most important amateur contest - the ABA heavyweight final against Welshman Rudi Pika at Wembley in 1980. I just did enough to win and to prove to Terry Lawless that I had what it takes to make it in the professional game

Nobody puts a gun to my head and makes me box. I do it because I enjoy it and it's helping me become a somebody instead of an out-of-work nobody, know what I mean?

Anyway, as I was saying about the building site - it was murderously hard work and I used to be so tired when I got home that I could hardly raise any energy for training. I later got a much cushier job serving in a Lonsdale sports shop, and I was able to give my training and boxing the serious attention it needed. My amateur career lasted a couple of seasons and I had twenty-one contests. The one and only defeat came in my third bout when I was matched out of my depth against experienced Irish international Joe Christle. I came very close to being stopped in that one. He knew too many tricks, and kept making me hit shadows while he hardly missed with a single punch.

Near the end of my amateur career I got my own back when I boxed Joe in a return match on his own manor in Dublin. I stopped him in two rounds and, lovely sportsman that he was, he put two big arms around me after he had recovered his senses and said: 'Well done, Frank. You're going to go a long long way in this game.'

I knew I was beginning to look the part because the sharp men in camel-hair overcoats and driving Rollers were starting to appear and whisper in my ear. But before I listened to what they had to say I first wanted to achieve something positive as an amateur so that when I went into the professional game I would be treated with respect right from the off.

After boxing for Young England I won through to the ABA finals where I met a tough-as-nails Welshman called Rudi Pika. We had a really hard battle. It was nothing classy. I think we were both too drained by nerves to produce our best form. I managed to land the cleaner punches, and nicked a points decision that gave me my happiest moment in amateur boxing.

Now I knew I was ready to turn pro, and somebody sitting at the Wembley ringside that night shared my view. He was not only to become the most important man in my life but like a second father to me.

The man was, of course, Terry Lawless.

4: My 'Second' Father

When you think of big-time boxing managers you get a picture in your mind of men in camel-hair coats, smoking cigars and driving Rollers. Terry Lawless is nothing like this. The next flash thing he does will be the first flash thing he has ever done. He has never made me a promise he hasn't kept and I would trust him with my life. I look on him as a second father.

The first time Terry spoke to me it was to congratulate me on winning the ABA heavyweight title at Wembley in 1980. He didn't try to sell himself when he spoke, but was sincere in telling me: 'With the right attitude, Frank, you can go all the way in this game. If you're thinking of turning professional I would like the opportunity to tell you what we could do together. Whatever you decide, good luck.'

That was it. There was no wild talk of the fortunes I could earn and he didn't try blowing his own trumpet when it could have been so easy for him, know what I mean, to point out his incredible record as a manager. But I knew all about him and couldn't help but be impressed by the way he had steered John Stracey, Maurice Hope, Jim Watt and Charlie Magri to world titles (Charlie's world crown came later, but he was already the No 1 contender for the flyweight championship).

I got a lot of approaches, some of the fellers offering me the earth - and the sun and the stars, too - to sign with them. I'd be a liar if I didn't admit I was tempted by some of the offers, but I knew I owed it to myself to hear what the top manager in the game, Terry Lawless, had to say before I made any decision.

We arranged to meet at his gymnasium over the Royal Oak pub in Canning Town which is real 'EastEnders' territory. I went along expecting to hear him trying to impress me with talk of what I could earn. Instead of that he painted a picture of how hard it was going to be for me. I can recall all that he said to me as if it were something I'd learnt off by heart, and I can also remember what was going through my mind as he talked to me....

'Listen,' he said, in that firm, quiet Cockney voice of his, 'I'm not going to - as the song goes - promise you a rose garden. There are a lot of thorns in the boxing business and you must be well aware of them before you take the plunge and sign as a professional. I'm sure you've had big offers of signing-on fees. Well that's not my way. Just bear in mind that the moment you take a whack of money from somebody they want it back at some stage with big interest.'

Yeah, that's true. I've got fellers offering me fortunes, but it's what they want in return that worries me, know what I mean? As Dad always used to say to me, 'Nobody gives you something for nothing in this world.'

'The only promise I'll make to you is that if you sign with me I shall give you the best possible preparation for your contests and I shall make sure you get the ring education you need. You've won the ABA heavyweight championship and that's a great feat. But amateur boxing is child's play compared with what you can expect as a professional.'

Three rounds is exhausting enough. I wonder what it's like to have to go ten or even fifteen rounds?

My manager, my mate. Terry and I show our mutual affection here like consenting adults. But Terry would like it to be known that we're just good friends!

'If you're looking for an easy way to the top then I suggest you look for it elsewhere, because if you join me I'll see to it that you work your backside off. Fitness is 75 per cent of the business. The rest is a mixture of talent, heart, determination, dedication and character. I think you've got the talent, but only you know in your heart whether you can give the necessary commitment.'

I'm ready to give it all I've got. Boxing is the only way out for me. Otherwise, God forbid, it's back to the building site.

'You're still a baby yet and I wouldn't be looking to rush you along. In my opinion, heavyweights don't get anywhere near their peak until their mid-20s. You're only eighteen and have all the time in the world on your side. I don't know what you're planning, but I would warn you to think very carefully before signing for any manager who is going to make you run before you can walk. You might pick up some quick money, but you could get to the top without having served a proper apprenticeship and then you could find yourself in big trouble because you haven't learned the trade properly.'

I know I've got a lot to learn about the game. If I'm going to make it as a pro, I've got to learn how to throw combination punches like the top Yanks and also how to pace myself. I'm now listening to the feller who could help teach me all these things 'cos he's done it all before.

'I'll let my record as a manager speak for itself but I want you to know that I've got the contacts and the connections to make sure you get the right platform for your career. I can help teach you everything you need to know. But you've got to be prepared to give me blood, sweat and tears in return.'

It's never been a secret that Terry worked closely with Mickey Duff and Mike Barrett, the top promoters in Europe. He could get me on the Wembley shows and one day I could even top the bill there.

'Have a think about what I've said and then let me know whether we can do

It's a frame-up. This portrait of me hangs in the National Gallery. It's the only time you'll see Terry and me smiling after I've been put on the canvas

business together. You've got a lot to learn, but I feel that with the right guidance you can go all the way. I can promise you my best attention provided you are ready to give me your best effort.'

That was it. No sales talk. No offers of flash cars, promises of golden purses or guaranteed title fights. The only real promise he'd made was that it was going to be a future of blood, sweat and tears.

I looked around the crowded, buzzing gymnasium. Ray Cattouse, British light-weight champion, was shadow boxing in one corner. Charlie Magri, European flyweight champion and No.1 contender for the world title, was doing floor exercises on the other side of the gym. Maurice Hope, world light-middleweight champion, was sparring in the ring, and just a few feet away world lightweight champion Jim Watt was admiring himself in the mirror (just joking, Jim).

Terry didn't need to give me a sales pitch. The evidence of what he could do for me was there in front of my eyes. Other managers had filled my ears with sweet talk about the millions they could make for me, but deep down I'm a suspicious, cautious sort of feller and I had alarm bells ringing in my head telling me to beware. I'd heard loads of stories about fighters being ripped

The bandaging of hands is a vital part of fight preparations. Terry is a master wrapper. Looking on, left, is my talented trainer Jimmy Tibbs

off by managers who cheated on their purses and appeared only on fight night. I told Terry that I would think things over but in my heart I already knew that he was the man for me.

In Terry Lawless I have found more than a manager. He's like a father confessor for me and I can go to him with any problem and he'll sit down and help me solve it. Mind you, he's not all sweetness and honey. He's given me a few rollockings that have made me quake in my shoes. But it's

always been for the right reasons and once he has had his say he drops the subject and gets on with the job in hand. He's a professional from the top of his head to the tip of his toes.

Terry is happiest when he is at his home in Emerson Park, Essex, with his lovely wife Sylvia and twenty-two-year-old son, Stephen, who has become one of my few close mates. Terry can be as tough as granite when it comes to business, but he melts and becomes like a big, soft, cuddly bear when his daughter, Lorraine, and son-in-law, Trevor, arrive with the apples of his eye - his two grandsons, Terry and Joseph. I feel it a privilege to be in his company when they are around because he

That's the way to do it! Terry is without doubt the best boxing coach in the game, and here he is telling me how I can improve my guard. When Terry talks, I listen and learn. He and trainer Jimmy Tibbs have taught me most of what I know

relaxes to the extent where he is just about the nicest person you could wish to meet.

All the tensions and pressures of big fight management - and believe me, these are enormous - drop off him and he has us rolling about with his quick humour and sunny smile. He and Sylvia have one of the strongest marriages I have ever come across. It's lasted thirty years so far, and I have been lucky enough to have been treated like a second son by them whenever I stay at their home during my preparation for fights. Sylvia spoils me with her superb cooking and can never do enough to make me feel at home. If she gets round to reading this book I hope she accepts my grateful thanks for all she has done for me. I'm not great with words and so probably don't express my appreciation like I should but I'd like her to know that all she does for me is not taken for granted.

One of the things I like most about Terry is his loyalty. He's got the same set of friends now that he had twenty or more years ago. Success has not spoiled him and provided you give him loyalty in return he will battle all the way for you. I often go to

Promoter Mike Barrett, pictured here with Terry and me, has played an important role in helping me get established on the world scene. Along with his internationally-famous partner, Mickey Duff, he has given me the impressive stages at Wembley and the Royal Albert Hall on which to learn and earn

Who's a pretty boy, then? Training is a serious business but Terry always finds time for a smile.

eat with him at his favourite East London restaurant, the Trattoria Parmigiana in Leytonstone, where he is usually surrounded by his close friends, Ken and Jean Gilliland, Tony and Babs Burns, Eileen Giller and her inquisitive husband, Sue and Les Falco and Les Eyres, his old mate from the days more than thirty years ago when he was working as a tally clerk in the docks. Les lost a leg in an accident at the docks and is always quick to tell people how Terry helped him out of a deep depression. That's typical of Terry. He's always looking to quietly help others.

His influence on me has been enormous. He is always quoting to me from books he has read and he encourages me to improve my reading. He has introduced me to the Japanese world of Zen, which is a mind-over-matter philosophy. It's not easy to grasp, but Terry patiently explains it to me and has got through to me about the importance of positive thinking. One of my great loves is listening to rock music (too loudly for Terry's taste), but he has got me interested in two of what he calls 'the greatest heavyweights of the century' -

opera singers Luciano Pavarotti and Placido Domingo - by occasionally slipping tapes onto my ghettoblaster. If Terry's dream were to come true, he would match them against each other in a double-header and have judges deciding which is the greater tenor. He has also made me aware of the importance of your appearance both in and out of the ring. 'If you take pride in the way you look outside the ring you will carry that pride into the ring with you,' he says in a way that tells you he obviously had the shiniest boots in his days as an Army sergeant when doing his National Service. I'm not one of the world's greatest spenders - the money is too hard earned to throw it around - but I like to buy smart clothes, and I was really proud to be named in a top-ten list of Britain's best-dressed men in the spring of 1986. That pleased Terry no end because it was positive proof that I had listened to his advice. As Terry always says: 'Be smart!'

Something else I like about Terry is that he never judges people by the colour of their skin. You can be white, black, yellow or pink and he will take you as he finds you. Like me, Terry believes that in the eyes of the Lord we are all created equal.

The only time I've ever known him ready to throw in the towel was when I lost to James 'Bonecrusher' Smith (I go into that fight in detail in the Scrap Album section). On the same nightmare night at Wembley Mark Kaylor was beaten by Buster Drayton. Terry told me that was it. He'd decided to jack it in. All the pressures had got on top of him and he said he was getting out of the fight game.

I pleaded with him to change his mind and told him that I wouldn't carry on without him. He decided to sleep on it and the next morning he was his old bouncing, confident self again. It brought home to me the pressure he carries every time one of his boxers climbs into the ring. He is caring and conscientious and puts the priorities of his fighters before everything else.

I know I wouldn't have achieved half of

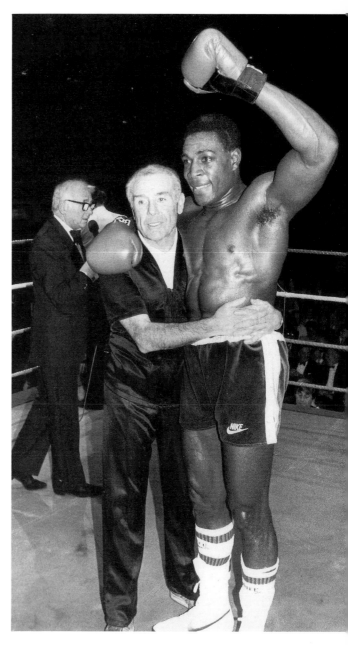

One of my favourite pictures of Terry and me. It was taken after my comeback victory over Ken Lakusta, which followed my crushing defeat by 'Bonecrusher' Smith. What we were hoping to get together was a hold on the world championship

what I have without his support and guidance. That's Terry Lawless. My manager. My mate.

5: The Bogata Connection

The worst day in my life, apart from the day my dad died, was when I went to the British Boxing Board of Control for a licence to box as a professional and was turned down. I failed their strict medical test.

It was Terry Lawless who gave me the bad news. The medical examination had revealed that I was short-sighted in my right eye. I could see clearly - certainly across the width of a ring - but to get a licence you need perfect vision.

I was heartbroken. It looked as if my career was finished before it had even started. Terry shared my disappointment but refused to sit back and just accept that my boxing days were over.

He took me to see a good friend of his, Mr David McLeod, a surgeon at the famous Moorfields eye hospital in London. He was the skilled surgeon who had saved Maurice Hope's career with an operation that meant he could carry on fighting as world champion. Mr McLeod gave me a thorough examination and then announced that my problem could be cured.

'There are two surgeons in the world performing an operation that cures myopia,' he said. 'That's the good news. The bad news is that one is in Moscow and the other in Bogota.'

Moscow? Bogota? I would have been prepared to go to the moon if it meant getting a licence to box as a professional.

Terry asked Mr McLeod to look into the possibility of me having the operation. Within a month he had arranged for me to go to Bogota as a patient, with Terry footing the bill out of his own pocket. That was astonishing proof of his faith in me.

'You're going to have to make the journey on your own, Frank,' he explained. 'I'll see to it that you are met at the airport when you get to Bogota.'

It was only then that it dawned on me that I had no idea where Bogota was. I looked it up in an atlas and found that it was the capital of Colombia, South America, on the other side of the world. It rang a bell with me, and when I asked Terry what the place meant to him he said: 'That was where Bobby Moore got arrested on a trumped-up jewel theft charge.'

This had been in 1970 when he was captain of the England World Cup team. They had stopped off in Colombia to play a warm-up match just before the World Cup finals in Mexico. Bobby Moore and Bobby Charlton had gone into a jewellery shop to look for gifts to take home to their wives, and after they had left one of the shop assistants claimed that Moore had nicked a gold bracelet.

Bobby was arrested and the team had to go on to Mexico without him. The charges were later dropped and he joined the squad in time to lead England to the quarter-finals. It came out at the time that Bobby had walked into what was known as the 'Bogota Boobytrap'. Apparently, it was commonplace for innocent tourists to be accused of stealing jewellery, and many of them used to pay up on the spot to avoid any hint of scandal.

'Whatever you do,' Terry warned, only half jokingly, 'don't go near any jewellery shops while you're out there. If you do, copy what Bobby Moore says he now does. Look in the window with your hands in your pockets and point at the jewels with your nose!'

28

I had only flown in a 'plane once before. That was on a short hop to Dublin with the Young England team. When Terry saw me off at Heathrow at the start of the twelve-hour flight in February, 1981, his final words were: 'Just do what you're told while you're out there and everything will be all right. You're going to a place where about only one in a million British people have ever been, so try to look on it as an adventure and enjoy the experience. If you're feeling at all homesick just pick up a 'phone and call me on reverse charges. It will all prove worthwhile, I promise you.'

I took Terry's advice and looked on it as a great adventure. And it was certainly that from the moment the jet took off. The flight seemed to last a lifetime, and when I finally got to Bogota there was nobody at the airport to meet me. So there I was in a strange land without a word of Spanish, and all I had on me was an envelope with the name of the hospital written on it. It took me about an hour to find anybody who could read it, and at last a cab driver agreed to run me there.

The person who was supposed to meet me at the airport, a travel agent's representative called Helen, finally caught up with me at the hospital and took me back into town where I stayed in a hotel for the first couple of nights. Then I went for an examination by Professor Jose Ignatio Barraquer, a world-famous eye surgeon who spoke only a little English. But he managed to say all that I wanted to hear. After looking into my eye through half a dozen different instruments, he beamed at me and said: 'This I can cure.'

I moved from the hotel to a sort of convalescence home half a mile from the hospital where there were patients from all over the world either recovering from or waiting to have eye operations by the enormously gifted professor. There was not a soul there who spoke English, but with a mixture of sign language and the use of a Spanish-phrase dictionary we all managed to understand each other and during my six-

Maurice Hope, the world light-middleweight champion whose career was saved by the skill of eye surgeon David McLeod. Mo will always have my admiration for the dignified way in which he carried the burden of being the first black immigrant to win a world boxing title for Britain. He was under enormous pressure but always behaved with impeccable sportsmanship. His favourite saying was: "Where there's life there's Hope."

29

Bobby Moore, who was caught in the Bogota Boobytrap. I made sure I gave the jewellery shops in Bogota a miss.

down about a mile from our destination and I finished up helping a couple of the other passengers push it while the driver shouted words of encouragement to us from behind the wheel. Some parts of Bogota where the rich people lived were beautiful, but on the other side of the city there was the worst poverty I have ever seen. There were a lot of beggars in the streets and the kids ran round wearing rags. It was a sight that sickened me, and it made me appreciate that where I was brought up in Wandsworth wasn't so bad after all.

At last it was time for my operation. I was on the operating table for several hours while I underwent something called - and here I'm relying on my ghostwriter to get the dictionary out - radial keratotomy. According to the distinguished professor, the procedure involved making small incisions in the cornea of my right eye to alter its shape. That's how it was explained to me anyway, with most of the medical terms going way over my head.

I spent the next six days with a patch covering my right eye. There was no pain, just a little discomfort. Then came the big day when the patch was removed and the professor made a thorough examination while beaming different strengths of light in my eye. After about half an hour he slapped me on the back and said: 'Everything is fine, young man. You can now embark on your boxing career.'

I telephoned the good news to Terry and a week later headed for home at the end of an adventure that I will never forget. Making that marathon journey on my own and having to spend six weeks as a stranger in a foreign land helped me learn how to stand on my own two feet, and I know the Frank Bruno who arrived back at Heathrow Airport was a more mature and stronger-minded person than the young Frank Bruno who had flown out six weeks earlier.

Now all I wanted to do was get the gloves on and start fighting for pay. But first I had to get through a storm of my own making.

week stay I made some good friends. Two in particular, an elderly man from El Salvador and a younger chap from Venezuela, helped the time pass by challenging me to games of chess, which I had learned to play at Oak Hall.

To keep fit I used to go for early morning runs and I also walked for miles which was another good habit that I had picked up at Oak Hall where long hikes were always being encouraged. One day I got a bus into the centre of Bogota. It broke

6: Learning the Hard Way

I've made only two serious mistakes since getting together with Terry Lawless. The second was forgetting to duck against Bonecrusher Smith. The first was allowing myself to be sweet-talked into agreeing to let somebody else be my manager.

I was bursting to get my career under way when I returned home from Bogota after my eye operation. Terry, acting on the expert advice of distinguished eye surgeon David McLeod, told me it would be six months before I could start proper training for my professional debut. That meant it would probably be at least a year before I could get into action. It seemed a lifetime away and I got really depressed.

It was sometime round about then that one of the managers who had been on my trail during my amateur days came back into my life. I found him a real charmer and I have to admit I was impressed by his Rolls-Royce and all the trappings that went with it which proved he was a wealthy and successful businessman.

The upshot of it was that during one of my meetings with him I signed a piece of paper without really realising the commitment I was making. Like I said right up front in this book, reading has never been my strongest point. Anyway that piece of paper came back to haunt me, and also to hit Terry in the pocket where it hurts.

The 'charmer' lost his charm and became furious when I made it clear that Terry Lawless was the man I wanted to manage me. There were a lot of nasty things said, but Terry protected me from much of the mud that was flying about. The argument finished up in court with a judge deciding that Terry should be my manager - which pleased me no end.

That was the good news. The bad news was that the judge ruled that the other manager had a possible claim for damages. The row rumbled on for three years and it was finally settled just before my European championship fight against Anders Eklund in October 1985. Terry agreed to settle out of court and, with legal costs included, the bill was reported in the newspapers to be in the region of a hundred thousand pounds. So the people who think he has earned a fortune with me should think again, know what I mean? Terry never brings up the subject of the costs with me. He doesn't think I should be burdened with anything that could take my mind off boxing matters and my target of becoming world champion.

I have always felt guilty and sorry for the aggravation I caused Terry. I had learned the hard way that you should never ever sign anything without realising the exact meaning of the words. If any young boxers with professional ambitions are reading this I urge them to learn from my bad experience and get somebody they can trust to study the small print before they put their signature to any kind of contract. Don't get blinded by Rolls-Royces and large mansions. If it's somebody looking to manage you, do your homework and find out exactly what he has achieved with other boxers. And remember, if you take a signing-on fee from him he will be looking to get that money back *plus* a healthy profit.

Anyway, Terry helped me close my mind to the problems I had caused and we got down to the serious business of

Jim Watt, former world lightweight champion and the idol of Scotland, who told me: "Only listen to good advice." I rated that good advice.

preparing for my professional debut. I passed the British Boxing Board of Control medical test without any trouble and six months after the eye operation I was allowed to put the gloves on and spar for the first time since deciding to turn professional.

Colin Hart, one of Terrys' close friends among the sports reporters, came and watched me work out and was the first to get an earful of one of my 'you know what I mean' interviews. He wrote a nice piece in *The Sun* about me being potentially the best British heavyweight for twenty years.

It was my first big write-up, but before I could get carried away by it Terry told me: 'Colin's a good judge and knows what he's talking about, but don't make the mistake that so many sportsmen make of believing your own publicity. You have still got it all to do and that means you are going to have to make a lot of sacrifices. I promise you that you're going to get a lot of headlines in the next few years because the country is crying out for a world-class heavyweight. But be prepared for knocks as well as praise from the press. We are the worst nation in the world for building up heroes and then knocking them down. So keep all that the newspapers write about you in perspective.'

It was all part of what Terry calls 'the education of Bruno'. I also learned valuable lessons before I had thrown a single punch as a professional by working out alongside Jim Watt, who was training to defend his world lightweight title against Sean O'Grady.

Jim was a remarkable fighter. He had been written off as virtually finished before joining Terry's stable at the age of twenty-seven and in four astonishing years won the European and world 9st 7lb titles. I have never known a perfectionist quite like Jim. He always knew his exact bodyweight to the nearest ounce and was almost scientific in his approach to his diet and fight preparation.

'Always remember, Frank,' he said to me once, 'boxing is a sport where you have to be completely single-minded. You get a lot of whisperers in this business, people talking in your ear about things they know

It's in the gym that I work to improve the delivery and variety of my punches. If anybody ever tells me that I get a lot of luck I use one of Terry's lines in reply: "The harder I work the luckier I get."

John Conteh, former world light-heavyweight champion, was one of my schoolboy heroes. He was without doubt one of the most talented fighters Britain has ever produced. His world title victory against Jorge Ahumada at Wembley in 1974 - when I was just dreaming of becoming a world champion - gave me tremendous incentive

I also remember Jim Watt's company in the gymnasium because of his sense of humour. There was the time when I had just got a new motorcar - well, more of a new secondhand one. Jim arrived for a training session and said to me all serious-faced: "I hate to have to tell you this, Frank, but there's a dirty big chip on the bonnet of your car."

I rushed downstairs to where I'd parked it and there on the bonnet was a potato chip.

A few days later I was a walk-on guest when Eamonn Andrews surprised Jim with the 'This Is Your Life' book. Another of the guests was former world light-heavyweight champion John Conteh, who was second in line only to Muhammad Ali as my boxing idol when I was at school. I am trying to live up to the great boxing standards that John set, but I am not following the sort of life-style that he led. I suppose there are some people who would consider me a bore because I'm a non-drinker, a non-smoker and the so-called bright lights do nothing for me. I know from the hundreds of letters I get every week that a lot of youngsters look up to me and I will always do my best to set them the best possible example.

It pleases me to see John Conteh looking back on top of the world. He was a magnificent fighter at his peak but I think he could have done with some of that advice that Jim Watt passed on to me: *"Only listen to good advice."*

little about. Listen to Terry and your trainers and shut most of the others out. My advice is "only listen to good advice."'

I rated that as good advice and have tried to follow it.

I was learning the hard way but the education of Bruno was improving me all the time, making me better as a fighter and stronger and wiser as a man. Now all I had to do was prove I could fight in the ring where it really mattered.

7: The A (for 'Appy') Team

My favourite television programme is 'East-Enders'. I probably enjoy it more than most people because I take part in the *real* thing nearly every day.

The Royal Oak pub in Canning Town over which Terry Lawless has his gymnasium could easily be the Queen Vic that features in every episode of East-Enders. It is packed with great characters who could have walked off the set.

There's a small market place and parade of shops directly opposite which is just like Albert Square. I'm always popping over there to buy bags of fruit and drinks, and consider the stallholders and shopkeepers as mates. They are always cheerful and full of words of encouragement, and their humour is something special. 'You can do it, my son,' they say before a fight. 'Give him one for me while you're about it.'

Everywhere you go there is good humour and the sort of matiness that you find only in the East End. Mind you, upstairs in the Royal Oak it's strictly business although we do find time when we're not sweating and straining to have a good laugh. Johnny Speight, creator of Alf Garnett, dropped in recently and had us rolling about with true East End stories. One was told to him by actor Terence Stamp, who was born and raised in the East End. A retired docker, a real Alf Garnett type, was sitting at the kitchen table reading the racing pages while his wife struggled to get the fire alight. The gasman happened to be there reading the meter and said to the old girl: "Ere, I'll do that for you love.' As he raked the fire with the poker all the coal fell into the grate. The husband peered over the top of his paper and said: 'I could have f-----g done that!'

One reason for the success of Terry Lawless as Britain's leading boxing manager is the way he has the gymnasium organized. There can often be a dozen or more top professional fighters working out in what is a fairly confined space but because all the training programmes are planned to the last detail there is never any hassle. To satisfy the Lawless demands every one of his fighters has to become a fitness fanatic. You will never find fitter fighters anywhere in the world than those from the Royal Oak 'EastEnders' stable.

Terry, the Master, is in overall command and has trainers Jimmy Tibbs and Frank Black as the best back-up team in the business. Frank, who used to be a footballer on Millwall's books, has been with Terry for more than fifteen years and knows the big fight routine inside out. A staunch Roman Catholic who often comes with me to church, Frank has lived on the east side of London for most of his life but still has the thick accent of his Irish homeland. He must take a lot of credit for my physical fitness because he is the man who pushes me through my vital ground-exercises programme.

The trainer who works most with me is Jimmy Tibbs, who was a championship contender in his days as a professional light-heavyweight before he got dragged into a family feud that ended with him spending some time 'resting' at Her Majesty's pleasure, know what I mean? He was highly respected for the skill and speed of his punching combinations, and has helped me no end by putting on the coaching pads and encouraging me to improve the accuracy and variety of my punches. There is 'the Tibbs touch' to nearly

The A (for 'Appy) Team from left to right: Frank Black, guess who, Terry Lawless and Jimmy Tibbs. Terry reckoned the wig in this Daily Mail *picture by Monty Fresco fitted me to a 'T'*

The A (for 'Appy) Team as we really are. Frank Black (left) and Jimmy Tibbs are two of the best trainers in the business and I owe them both a big vote of thanks

everything I do in the ring, and I will always be grateful to him for all the effort he has put in to make me a more formidable fighter.

Another familiar figure at the gym is George Wiggs, an old timer who has been a member of the training team almost as long as Terry has had a manager's licence which is nearly thirty years. Another important man in helping me to get prepared for a fight is Rupert Doaries. I call him 'The Man with the Magic Hands.' He's a masseur and I go to him three or four times a week at West Ham Baths to have a 30-minute massage that keeps my muscles nice and loose.

This is a typical daily timetable for me when I'm into the final weeks of my preparation for a fight:

6.30 a.m.: I'm always up with the birds. It's my favourite time of the day. I slip into a Nike tracksuit and size 11 Nike training shoes and leave the house as quietly as possible so as not to wake Laura, the lady in my life, and our gorgeous three-year-old daughter Nicola. I often fail and spend ten minutes talking to Nicola in her cot. Shortly before seven o'clock I get behind the wheel of my Granada Ghia, switch on a tape of a rock band with all six stereo speakers blasting out nice and loud and then take the ten-minute drive to the edge of Hainault Forest. For forty-five minutes I run through the woods, sometimes with talented European feather-weight champion Jim McDonnell as my running partner. We don't try to race each other. We're not trying to be the next Seb Coe and Steve Ovett. The idea is to run stamina and strength into our legs because these are every bit as important to a boxer as his fists. Rocky Marciano, the only world heavyweight champion to retire without a single defeat on his record, was once asked which was his most important weapon and he surprised the interviewer by saying: 'My legs.' I understand what The Rock meant because once your legs go tired you are unable to avoid the punches coming at you. I usually run seven miles a day during the week and five miles on Saturday and Sunday. I can't tell you how good it feels to be out running first thing every morning, even in the depth of winter. The air is fresh and clean and I enjoy seeing the rabbits, squirrels and birds going about their business as nature intended. I suppose without knowing it my five years at Oak

It's hard graft in the gym but we do find time for laughs. This is former world flyweight champion Charlie Magri and me taking off Little and Large

Trainer Jimmy Tibbs pulls on the coaching pads during every one of my training sessions and we work on sharpening new combination punches and at improving old ones. Jimmy was a top-flight professional and really knows the ropes

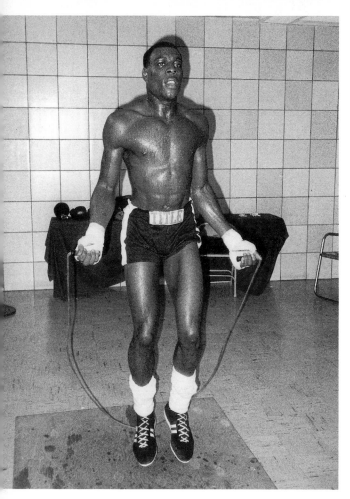

Salt...mustard...vinegar...pepper. Skipping helps keep your leg muscles supple and gives you vital rhythm. I have two skipping sessions every day

Hall must have turned me into something of a country boy at heart.

8.00 a.m.: I arrive home for a brisk twenty minute work out in the small gym that I have set up in my garage. I do a quick burst of fast rope skipping followed by some weight-training lifts (I deliberately say weight*training* because weight*lifting* can harm boxers by giving them muscles that are bunched and tight and not loose and supple like they need to be). Then I thump a heavy bag (goodness knows what my neighbours think, but they have yet to complain), and finish with combination punches on the speedball. Finally I have a shower and think hungrily of breakfast.

8.45 a.m.: Breakfast, with Laura doing the cooking and me the eating. I start off with a cereal, followed by a medium-cooked large steak, three fried eggs - sunny side up - half a dozen sausages, and bacon and fried tomatoes. You try running seven miles every morning. It does wonders for your appetite. I finish off with a couple of rounds of toast and a pint of fresh orange juice. I'm not being a pig. I am just stoking up energy for what lies ahead.

9.45 a.m.: I walk our two Doberman dogs, Bomber and a bitch called Angie - named after my favourite character in 'EastEnders'. Just so that I don't get lazy I put on specially weighted ankle bracelets and sometimes I wear a waistband weighing 100 pounds.

10.30 a.m.: To bed for an hour. I just doze and get my thoughts working. Terry has taught me to be a positive thinker and I lie on the bed picturing in my mind's eye how I am going to win the heavyweight championship of the world. I never allow myself to have negative thoughts. Quite often I will open the Bible at any page and read a few passages. I find it comforting. Let me try it this second. The page has fallen open at Proverbs, chapter 4, verse 14*: Enter not into the path of the wicked, and go not in the way of evil men.* Now there's food for thought.

12.30 p.m.: The Royal Oak gym. I strip off my tracksuit and cover myself all over with cocoa butter-oil. It is a habit I picked up during a visit to the States when I noticed all the Latin-American boxers doing it in the New York gym where I trained. I

The water baby! Some people might think I'm more like a water buffalo. I like a slow, lazy swim and often put in twenty or more lengths. If I'm in the late stages of training I spend only about twenty minutes in the water each day. It doesn't do to get too loose, know what I mean?

On yer bike! I pedal for miles without getting anywhere, but the exercise does my legs a power of good

Terry told me I had to be prepared to give blood, sweat and tears . Well, here's the sweat. You have to perspire if you want to aspire.

find it helps me sweat more and it makes me feel sleek and supple. For ninety minutes - with Frank Black motivating me - I will follow a series of explosive floor exercises, mixed in with skipping, a session on the bike machine, shadow boxing, punching the heavy bag and the speedball. I then work on new moves and punch patterns with Jimmy Tibbs who will wear large flat coaching pads on his hands. Finally, with Jimmy and Terry watching carefully and calling out instructions, I will spar for up to 12 rounds. It used to be really hard to find sparring partners but the gym is now creaking under the weight of my heavyweight stablemates Adrian Elliott, Gary Mason and new British heavyweight king Horice Notice. They all willingly spar with me and for the three weeks building up to a fight Terry imports highly-paid sparring partners - usually from the United States. I am allowed to unload my heavy ammunition against them because they are getting well compensated out of my pocket.

3.30 p.m.: I cross the road from the gym and buy two bananas, a pound of grapes, an orange and an apple from Wally, the greengrocer. Then I buy a bottle of Lucozade and sit in the car while I eat the fruit and guzzle the drink. Half an hour later I arrive at West Ham Baths where I have a twenty-minute swim, a session in the vapour room and then a relaxing massage from Rupert Doaries.

6.00 p.m.: Time for dinner after I've had a playful romp with Nicola. Laura does the cooking, me the eating (or, if it's in the final two weeks before a contest I stay at the Lawless home where Sylvia takes over as my cook). I like half a chicken with salad followed by a large steak, a mountain of mixed vegetables and two pints of orange juice. It will not surprise you to learn that my food bill runs at something around £150 a week

7.30 pm: After taking the dogs for another stroll I go to bed where I watch fight videos of the all-time great champions for a couple of hours. My favourites are Joe

Louis and Muhammad Ali. It's difficult to pick which one of them was The Greatest but it definitely rests between these two with Rocky Marciano just behind, mainly because he did not have sufficient bodyweight. I am more of a Louis than an Ali in my style. To be a big puncher you have to plant your feet on the canvas the way Louis did. Ali was an up-on-the-toes dancer and was rarely an explosive puncher because he was usually on the move as his blows landed. A lot of his punches had just his arm-weight behind them, whereas Louis used to follow through and get all his body behind his punch. I have always believed in the big follow-through when throwing a punch. With these sort of tactical thoughts in my mind I fall asleep dreaming of following my heroes Louis and Ali as heavyweight champion of the world. My sex life takes a back seat when I'm in full training.

There are some sportsmen who claim they thrive on having sex shortly before their competitions, but I belong to the school that thinks it's better to go without. I switch off three weeks before every fight. I couldn't believe it when my former stablemate Lloyd Honeyghan admitted that he had made love on the night before he fought for the British championship. It obviously didn't affect his performance in the ring because he was a conclusive winner, but it certainly isn't the way I would approach a fight. The life I lead is a tiring and lonely one. I don't have many close friends my own age simply because I have to shut off from everybody and concentrate in a single-minded way on my target of one day winning the world heavyweight championship. As Terry Lawless warned me right from the start, to get to the top you have to make sacrifices. Believe me, getting there is sheer hard work.

Before I know it the alarm is signalling that it's 6.30 a.m. and I'm off on another full day of training. And I love every second of it.

Another training session over and the cameraman catches me taking a one-eyed view of the world. But I have both eyes fixed firmly on that world heavyweight crown

I'm under wraps at the end of another tough work-out. I know the harder I work in training the easier it will be when I get into the ring

8: At the Camp of King Larry

I sat alongside the then undefeated world heavyweight king Larry Holmes at one of the hotels he owns near his palatial home in Easton, Pennsylvania, waiting to hear words of advice on how I could one day follow him as champion. 'Listen young, man,' he said, raising a forefinger to emphasize his point, 'and listen good. Whatever you do *stay off the coke.'*

I think my mouth dropped open with astonishment. I had been expecting to hear something about keeping my guard up or getting behind my punches but here he was talking about drugs. Terry and famous international promoter Mickey Duff had taken me to see Holmes during a 1983 'education of Bruno' trip to the United States. The champ had gone out of his way to impress us, giving us a tour of his business empire in Easton which could have been called Holmesville. There was a street named after him and it seemed he had a piece of the action in nearly every corner of the small town. He proudly showed us his name emblazoned across restaurants, hotels, discos, car parking lots and offices.

We did the tour with King Larry in the grand manor, being driven in an enormous white Cadillac with solid gold fittings, and a cocktail cabinet and television in the back. During the hour-long drive Larry and his two bodyguards must have called up and talked to a dozen different people on their walkie-talkie sets. To be completely honest, I was not that impressed by the set-up of which Larry was so proud. I thought it was all a bit flash and over-the-top, but that's the way they like to do things in America and you could not help but admire what Larry had achieved for himself from poor beginnings.

It was when we returned to Larry's hotel that he gave me the warning about the dangers of drugs. 'The evil drug pushers have infiltrated the world of boxing over here in the States,' he said. 'The game is full of cocaine sniffers. It makes me want to weep to see so many of the kids getting into the stuff.'

He looked at me real hard, know what I mean? 'Now I'm telling you for your own good,' he said, 'don't have anything to do with it. It's no use me, or Terry or Mickey here, advising you how to block a left lead or throw a right cross if you're going to go off and ruin it all by sniffing coke. Remember, you've gotta leave the stuff alone.'

I appreciated the advice but I had made a decision long before meeting King Larry that I would never have anything to do with the drugs scene. I know Terry feels just as strongly as I do about it. I want any youngster reading this to make a silent promise now never to touch drugs. They just become a crutch and one day you find you can't function without them. I've thought up this little slogan that you might want to pass on to anybody you know tempted to try them: *'Only mugs touch drugs.'*

The most memorable part of my trip to the Holmes camp was when we worked out together in the superbly-equipped gymnasium that he had built in the grounds of his home. He is one of the greatest left jabbers in the history of the game and gave me some useful tips on how to plant the jab solidly and with a final turn of the wrist that gives it extra power on impact. The one thing he wouldn't do, though, was spar with me. 'I ain't gonna have no kids trying out their

Here I am at the camp of King Larry, shaping up to the then world champion in the gymnasium that he has built in the grounds of his palatial home. We didn't get round to swapping punches. "You ain't gonna practice your punches on my head," said Larry. "My days as a sparring partner ended long ago."

punches on me,'he said. 'I've got better things to do with my head.'

Before leaving him, Larry took me on one side and told me: 'You could easily be my successor one day, Frank. You've definitely got the potential but don't be in no rush. You're young yet and should have as many easy fights as you can. Just two things - relax more in the ring. At the moment you're a little too stiff. The other thing is, like I say, stay off the coke.'

During that trip to the United States I had a ten-day training stop-over at the world-famous Grossingers camp up in the Catskill Mountains in New York State where I came across the most extraordinary character I have ever met in my life. Grossingers is where Rocky Marciano always used to train for his world title fights, and as I'm something of a nut about heavyweight boxing facts and figures I could almost feel the tradition of the place. We stayed in log cabins and I went on the same runs and worked out in the same gymnasium as the legendary Marciano did thirty years earlier.

There were two other heavyweight hopefuls there, big, strong black Americans called James 'Quick' Tillis and Jeff Sims. They didn't know what to make of me. I was the same size, the same colour but I

*The King and I. I learnt a lot from Larry,
particularly about his gift of the jab. Here he's
Holmes sweet Holmes.*

talked with what to them was a strange
accent, and they kept looking at me out of
the corners of their eyes during the first
couple of days when we used to sit together
at the large lunch table. Since my Oak Hall
days I have always prided myself on my
manners and make a point of saying 'please'
and 'thank you'. My politeness obviously
had an unsettling effect on Sims, who took
Terry Lawless on one side and said: 'This
guy Bruno, is he a faggot?'

Terry laughed out loud and replied:
'He's about as much a pouf as Sylvester
Stallone.' That helped them accept me and
for ten days we became good mates despite
trying to get the better of each other in tough
sparring sessions. Tillis, who always wore
a large cowboy hat, was quite a character
but it is Sims who I'll never forget. Peter
Batt, known as the 'Poet of Fleet Street' and
one of the brilliant scriptwriters who has
brought the 'EastEnders' to life, was at the

camp with us and just couldn't believe the
things he was hearing from Sims. 'If I put it
all down in a novel the publishers would
say it was too much fantasy,' he said.

I knew Sims, then twenty-nine and
ranked No 11 heavyweight, was something
different from the first minute of our
opening sparring session. I dropped him on
the seat of his pants with the first right hand
that I threw. He sat on the canvas and said
in a deep drawl: 'S-h-e-e-t. That chain gang
done slowed me down more than I
thought.'

Later on over dinner I asked him what he
meant about the chain gang. It turned out
that he had four bullets still wedged in him
from two shooting incidents plus scars from
forty stitches following knife fights. He
had served seven years in jail, most of them
on a chain gang, for shooting dead a man
who had previously shot him. Sims had
never known his father and from the age of
seven had travelled the South with his
mother and ten brothers and sisters, all of
them working for a share cropping gang.
He started boxing while in jail and became

prison champion of the State of Florida. It was his boxing that got him remission from a fifteen-year sentence and he turned professional on his release and won nineteen straight knockout victories. This was how Sims continued his remarkable story and to really appreciate it you have to remember that he was speaking with a sort of Deep South drawl:

'I'd got myself noticed and, man, I was living high on self respect for the first time in my life. Then my manager goes and matches me with another young world title

This is me cornered by the 'Grossinger Gang', as we were labelled by writer Peter 'The Poet' Batt who is on the extreme right of this picture that was taken by John Dawes for the Daily Star. *Top international promoter Mickey Duff is on the left with Terry Lawless, and James 'Quick' Tillis and Lloyd Honeyghan are alongside them. The unforgettable Jeff Sims is the one wearing the white brimmed hat*

contender. To save on expenses, the manager got both of us to live together while training. I ain't kiddin' you, man. The most important fight of my life and I'm having to sleep in the same room as my opponent. Anyways, one night we got to arguing over who should do the dishes and shift the garbage. We start to fight and then the next thing I knows he's got a gun out and is pointing it right at me. He pulled the trigger three times and I got hit in the shoulder, the ribs and the thigh. As I lay on the floor I heard him reloading and I thought, s-h-e-e-t, the son of a bitch is gonna finish me off. I dragged myself up and jumped two storeys out of the window. When I got outta hospital three weeks later I still had them slugs buried in me, plus another from when I got shot years earlier.'

I decided not to tell him the story of my days growing up in Wandsworth and going to Oak Hall because it might have convinced

him I really was a faggot!

Late one night during our second week at the camp we had the worst storm I've ever known in my life. Lightning hit a tree right outside our window and set it on fire, and a power cut plunged the entire camp into darkness. It rained so hard I thought we were all going to get washed away. When the rain stopped I followed Terry on a

Mike Weaver and I take a break during a training session. Mike, built like a weight-lifter, had a brief reign as world champion after knocking out Gerrie Coetzee in thirteen rounds in South Africa

stumbling journey through the pitch-black grounds to our cabin. It was pretty scarey, I can tell you. As I passed Jeff's door I noticed that his door was wide open. I peered in to his darkened cabin and found him lying stark naked on his bunk, staring dreamily off into space as if he didn't have a care in the world. 'Ain't you scared in there on your own, Jeff?' I asked, only half joking.

He didn't blink an eyelid as he replied: 'It don't worry me none, man. I done used to solitary.'

There was a definite unhinged side to

Sims, who had a favourite word that he kept using. At first I thought it was four words. It sounded like 'wreck a car ration.' It then dawned on me that it was one word, recreation. In the middle of one night he came banging on the door of my log cabin shouting: 'Come out, Bruno. It's time for our showdown. Let's get it on right here and now.'

I ignored him but was really angry to have my sleep interrupted. I gave him a right mouthful the next morning and he found out that there were times when I could forget to be polite. He put two big arms around me and hugged me. 'S-h-e-e-t man,' he said, 'I was only having a little rec-a-reation.'

During my education trip I worked out with Mike Weaver and Michael Spinks, a former and a future world heavyweight champion. Another sparring session was arranged with a young, up-and-coming American prospect called Mike Tyson. He was a powerful, bull-necked fighter with a lot of class, but I felt I gave as good as I got in a hard work-out. Only a handful of people were in the gym to watch us. "One day you two could be fighting for the world heavyweight championship with millions of eyes on you," said Mickey Duff. I also met promoter Don King, the 'Mr Boxing' of the United States who, if it's possible, is an even more unbelievable character than Jeff Sims. He once served time on a man-slaughter charge, and he talks like somebody who has swallowed a dictionary. His influence on the world boxing scene runs really deep, and his electric shock of hair is worn just like a crown that he is possibly entitled to wear as the king of the fight game.

The highspot of my trip was a two-round knockout victory over Mike Jameson in Chicago. It proved that the 'educating of Bruno' was bringing the right results.

Things were really moving for me and I had no time to spare for rec-a-reation.

Michael Spinks was world light-heavyweight champion when this picture was taken during my educational trip to the United States. He has since caused one of the biggest upsets in boxing history by taking the heavyweight crown from the previously undefeated Larry Holmes

Don King, who wears his hair like a crown. He is America's Mr Boxing and his influence runs right through the world heavyweight division.

9: Me and Our 'Enery

No doubt about it, Henry Cooper is still the biggest idol in British boxing despite the fact that it's more than fifteen years since he hung up his gloves. He had such charisma inside and outside the ring that his popularity has never been dented. If I could become a hero on anything like his scale I would feel as if I have really achieved something with my life.

Nowadays Henry keeps in touch with boxing through a newspaper column and with his inter-round summaries during fight commentaries on BBC radio. He's given me quite a bit of stick since I turned pro and a lot of people seem to think there is bad feeling between us. Well a lot of people are wrong.

The way I see it, Henry's got a job to do putting his views across to readers and listeners and it's his right to say exactly what he thinks. I have no recollection of Henry (or 'Enery as he's known to everybody) the boxer. He retired in March 1971 after losing a British, Commonwealth and European championship contest against Joe Bugner. I was just nine at the time and didn't get round to seeing him box, although I have watched him many times in recent years on video.

Looking at him in his contests against Muhammad Ali and Joe Bugner, Henry seemed a little too stiff and upright - which, funnily enough, is one of the criticisms he has made of me. I'm sure 'Enery will accept that I am entitled to my opinion just as much as he is. He had a good, solid jab and a helluva left hook but his right didn't seem anything to write home about.

But nobody can argue about the fact that he is loved by the British public, and I just hope I can keep everybody on my side long after I have retired just like 'Enery has done. He came down to the Royal Oak once to watch me train and get some facts for his newspaper column. I found him to be a lovely feller, and he said that I was 'a big, strong boy'. I listen with respect to what he has to say but I don't always agree with him. He has often had a go about the standard of my opponents but he should know better than anybody that the fight game is a hard old business and you don't try to learn the trade against the best men around. It's a harsh but true fact that all heavyweight champions finally become somebodies by fighting a lot of nobodies on the way. Remember Joe Louis's 'Bum A Month' campaign?

Anyway, as I was saying, I like our 'Enery and hope that I can represent boxing with the same pride and dignity that he has always shown. He continues to be a credit to a game that gets too much stick from people who don't know what they're talking about.

Floyd Patterson, one of Cooper's old rivals, came down to the Royal Oak gym one week at Terry's invitation to pass on some tips. We didn't have time for many sessions but we were together long enough for him to be able to give me some good advice about improving my weight balance and snapping rather than pawing with my left jab.

Floyd was the youngest-ever world heavyweight champion at twenty-one and became the first man to regain the crown in 1960 after knocking out Swedish idol Ingemar Johansson in a return title fight. I was grateful for all that he tried to teach me

Our 'Enery was a welcome visitor to the Royal Oak gymnasium to watch me training. 'Enery said in that lovely way of his: "He's a big, strong boy."

but, to be honest, I much prefer being taught and trained by Terry Lawless and Jimmy Tibbs because they speak my language, know what I mean?

I can usually take criticism in my stride but one feller who I thought went right over the top was Joe Frazier, the former world heavyweight champion who had three marvellous battles with Muhammad Ali. Smokin' Joe saw me just the once, in the only contest in which I was taken the distance on my way to a shot at the world title. It was against his fellow American Phil Brown at Wembley in 1984.

Brown had come only to survive and it was a bit of an untidy fight. Frazier jumped in with the view that I had only one style -

and that was no style at all. 'The guy is like one of those robot dolls with a big key in the back,' he told Bill Clark of the *Sunday Mirror*. 'He's a bomb that never explodes. He has more chance of being voted Mister America than of winning my old title.'

I have only respect and admiration for all that Smokin' Joe achieved in the ring and it hurt me that a man I looked up to could be so vicious with his tongue on the evidence of just one look at me. I would love to have listened to some good constructive criticism from him because I would have tried to learn from it, but he just went in with both hands as in his fighting days and seemed to want to tear me apart with hurtful words.

At least I wasn't rushed into a world title fight like his son, Marvis, who was way out of his depth when he challenged Larry Holmes in only his eleventh professional fight. Marvis was bombed out in the first round. That didn't seem like very good

Smokin' Joe Frazier, a fighter I greatly admire. But after just one look Joe didn't rate me at all. For once, Joe struck the wrong chord with me

Floyd Patterson gave me a hand with my training and I was honoured to take some tips from the man who, at 21, was the youngest world heavyweight champion of all time

matchmaking by his dad and manager, Smokin' Joe. Still, nobody will be able to take away from old Joe that he was one of the greatest heavyweight champions of all time. I just hope that one day I can earn from him the sort of respect that I have for all that he achieved in the ring.

One thing you have to do when you set your sights on being a successful sportsman, particularly in Britain, is grow a second skin because there is always an army of critics around who seem to delight in trying to pull you down. You have to turn a blind eye and cock a deaf ear to some of the spiteful things that are said and written about you. When people have booed me from the ringside I've just tried to look past them and not let them get under my skin.

Confidence plays a big part in the make-up of any champion. Climbing into the ring without confidence would be like getting in there naked. You've got to believe in yourself and not let the knockers unsettle you. The Bible puts it best - Isaiah, chapter 30, verse 15: *In quietness and confidence shall be your strength*. The likes of Ian Botham, Glenn Hoddle, Steve Davis and Daley Thompson will know what I mean about not letting the snipers get you down. Like them, I've had more than my share of knocks, but I just know that as long I can satisfy myself that I am doing my very best then my critics can go and take a running jump. I hope that doesn't make me sound flash but it's just the way I feel, know what I mean?

50

10: "Fanks Very Much, 'Arry"

There's Cannon and Ball, Little and Large, The Two Ronnies....and now a new television double act: Carpenter and Bruno. It seems that Harry Carpenter's BBCtv interviews with me have put us high in the comedy ratings.

Almost every impressionist on television puts me into their act, saying things like: 'Fanks very much, 'Arry'....and, of course, 'Know what I mean, 'Arry?' I used to say 'y'know' at the end of every sentence, and I made a real effort to stop myself and then found that I had replaced it with 'Know what I mean?' It's like a punctuation mark in my speech and I'm now stuck with it, know what I mean?

I know I make a right mess of the English grammar book, but I am sure the public would prefer me to speak and act naturally rather than put on an act. I've made a big effort to improve my vocabulary but my Cockney accent will be with me for all time. And I ain't making any apologies. I find it really comfortable talking to Harry Carpenter, who doesn't dig you in the ribs with questions but quietly encourages you to say what you feel. He was kind enough to say that I was the hardest-hitting British heavyweight he has seen, which is quite a compliment because he has been around the fight scene for more than thirty years and has reported on all the great post-war champions.

I've got so used to Harry waiting for me with a microphone in his hand at the end of fights that I must have seemed rude after my first-round victory over Gerrie Coetzee in a world title fight eliminator at Wembley. I was surprised to find Des Lynam waiting for me in the corner, and the first thing I said with millions of people listening in was: 'Where's 'Arry?' Sorry, Des. It was nothing personal, but I suppose I've come to look on 'Uncle' Harry as something of a lucky mascot.

The cruellest, yet in some ways the best take-off of me is on 'Spitting Image'. Some people seem to think I should feel insulted because of the way they portray me, but I laugh at it as much as anybody else, and feel flattered that they have considered me important enough to spend a lot of money making a dummy of me (There are some critics, notably Joe Frazier, who reckon I'm a dummy in the ring!)

I promise you I ain't no dummy like they present me on 'Spitting Image'. A lot of people who are supposed to be brainy don't really have any direction in life. Well, I know exactly where I'm going and I've learned to make the most of what gifts God has given. He didn't bless me with the sort of intelligence that you need to become a college professor, but I didn't do badly when it came to receiving the gift of a powerful physique. I came to terms very early in life with the fact that I was going to have to make my fortune by doing something physical. I wasn't born with a silver spoon in my mouth. I've had to do it all with my hands and, despite what you might think, quite a lot of brain power.

When you're up there in the ring it's like being an animal in the jungle. You've got to be quick witted and cunning as well as strong to survive.There's no place to hide and so you have to use your skill and think fast to get yourself out of trouble.

These ain't the words of the ghostwriter. This is me, Bruno, talking, and I'm telling

Our 'Enery and me make Harry Carpenter shoulder arms. Harry was a boxing reporter on the Daily Mail *way back when Henry was just starting out as an amateur. So I really respect his judgement, know what I mean 'Arry?*

you that boxers have an intelligence all their own. It's not the sort you get out of books. It's a sort of natural, instinctive intelligence. You have to out-think your opponent. It's like physical chess, but instead of moving pawns you move your fists and instead of going for checkmate you are looking for a knockout. Chess happens to be one of my favourite games so I know about these things, see!

Something else you need to be in the ring is brave. You'll never hear me bad-mouthing one of my opponents because I respect them. I know the courage it takes just to climb through the ropes. I listen to some of the terrible things that spectators shout from the safety of their seats and I want to go up to them and say: 'Oi, you, when did you have the guts to climb into the ring and face an opponent who wants to knock your block off?' Ninety-nine times out of a hundred the fellers who are shouting the loudest insults have never had a glove on in their lives. I know that for sure because anybody who has had the experience of getting up into the ring and giving and taking punches would not lower themselves to shout insults. They know the special person you have to be to get into the ring in the first place.

I'll be honest. I used to shake with nerves before my early amateur contests. It wasn't fear of getting hurt. Blimey, nobody could whack me as hard as my Dad used to with the curtain rod when I was misbehaving as a kid, so there was nothing for me to fear when it came to pain. What I used to be frightened of - and still am to a certain extent - is making a fool of myself by not performing at my best. Just imagine yourself climbing into the ring with the spotlight on you and the eyes of thousands of spectators watching your every move. It can be quite - what's the word I want ghostwriter? - daunting. Yeah, that's the word. Daunting.

I now thrive on it. It sets my adrenalin flowing, and when I climb through the ropes I am like a hand-grenade with the pin about to be pulled. But then comes the toughest part. You've rehearsed every move in training and have got yourself as fit as a fiddle, but unlike an actor who can spout the same lines every night of the week on stage you have to go out and perfom against somebody who hasn't read your script.

How would Lord Olivier cope with delivering his lines if somebody was going to belt him one every time he tried to open his mouth? We're just like actors up there in the ring, but instead of delivering lines we're delivering punches. And nobody writes the words for us. We have to come up with our own lines.

The one time I got my lines badly wrong was against 'Bonecrusher' Smith. I went for a big grandstand finish, playing to the gallery instead of following the script Terry had given me which was: 'Just stay out of trouble in this last round and you've won it by a mile. Don't get involved. Box.'

I got involved and tried to go for a knockout and was punished by getting knocked out myself for (please God) the one and only time in my career. Yet I now know that the defeat was the best thing that could have happened to me. It made a man of me overnight. It was God's way of telling me that I wasn't going to be given a world championship on a plate. I was going to have to battle for it with both my hands *and* all my heart. You would not believe the strength that I drew from that defeat. It broke Terry's heart more than mine. For me it wasn't the end of the world, more like a new beginning and I was able to pass my powerful belief on to Terry at a time when, for one of the few times in his life, he needed motivating. Looking back , I realise I was a boy when I went into the ring with 'Bonecrusher' and a man when I came out.

It was Harry Carpenter who reminded me that my idol Joe Louis had suffered his first defeat (by Max Schmeling) in his twenty-second fight. The 'Bonecrusher' set-back had come in my twenty-second fight and on what would have been Joe Louis's seventieth birthday. I thought about that and grew in confidence when I realised what Louis had achieved following his defeat. It was a fact well worth knowing. Fanks very much, 'Arry.

Would you say he's the Spitting Image of me? I reckon they have made a right pair of dummies out of 'Enery and me.

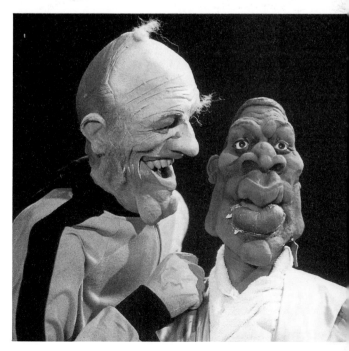

11: Ali - Still the Greatest

One of the most memorable yet saddest days of my life was when I met my idol, Muhammad Ali. We had a couple of hours together when he called to see me in my room at Caesar's Palace Hotel in Las Vegas where I was staying on the eve of the Hagler-Mugabi world middleweight championship contest.

There was a rat-a-tat-tat on my door and I could hardly believe my eyes when I opened it to see Ali standing there. Mickey Duff had told him I was in town and he kindly went out of his way to look me up. Or, as he put it, he had come to 'look me over.' Terry said it was a case of Muhammad coming to the mountain!

'I like to keep in touch with boxing folks from Britain,' Ali said as we warmly shook hands. 'I love the people of that country. They were right behind me throughout my career.'

It was memorable meeting for me because as far as I'm concerned Ali was - and still is - The Greatest. At his 'float-like-a-butterfly-sting-like-a-bee' peak there was nobody to touch him. What made it sad was to see him in less than good health. He suffers from Parkinson's Disease and is nothing like as sparkling and flamboyant as in his days as the world's undisputed number one personality.

The anti-boxing brigade try to put his condition down to the punches he took during his incredible career. But his illness could have struck him even if he had spent his life as a bus conductor punching tickets. There were still flashes of the old Ali when I called to see him. 'Man, I remember when I looked like you,' he said. 'That's a great physique you've got there. Mind you, I was much prettier. How old are you?'

'Twenty-four,' I told him.

'Twenty-four...why you're still a baby,' he said, no doubt remembering that when he was about the same age he was forced out of boxing for three and a half years for refusing to join the US Army and go to war in Vietnam.

He raised his fists in a playful sparring pose and came out with a touch of the old Ali patter: 'Let me tell you, if you can dance you've got a chance.'

But dancing is not my game in the ring. I prefer to plant both feet firmly on the canvas to make sure I'm getting full power into my punches. I've spent hours watching video replays of Ali at his greatest. If I lived to be 200 I couldn't learn to box in his style. I'm not a sweet-as-lollypops boxer in his or Sugar Ray Leonard's mould. Like I say, I stalk after opponents more in the style of another of my heroes Joe Louis.

I would have liked to box the Ali way, but you have to be born with his sort of athletic ability. Nobody could have taught him to box the way he did. It came to him as naturally as breathing.

Ali is one of the reasons I'm in the fight game. He captured my imagination when I was a kid, and it was dreaming of becoming a world champion like him that got me interested in putting on the gloves for the first time. I loved the way Ali turned himself into a showman. He had the fastest tongue in the west and made life easy for the reporters by filling their notebooks with marvellous quotes.

I couldn't begin to fight like him and

One of my all-time favourite photographs. Me with my idol Muhammad Ali. For me he is and always will be The Greatest. My thanks to ace Daily Mail *cameraman Monty Fresco for putting us in the picture*

A playful spar with The Greatest. He came up with a flash of the old Ali magic: "If you can dance, you've gotta chance."

neither could I talk like him. He shouted off his mouth but in a way that rarely gave offence. He wasn't a McEnroe; Ali amused rather than bruised with his tongue. He was an out-and-out entertainer. I was in awe of him when I finally met up with him in Las Vegas. In fact for the first few minutes of being in his company I was just about dumbstruck. There I was with a living legend and I could hardly get words out.

But he made me feel nice and relaxed and clowned around with me while *Daily Mail* photographer Monty Fresco took pictures

that have pride of place in my photo collection.

For me, Ali was and always will be The Man. The Cream. The Greatest.

A lesson I have learned from studying Ali's career is that you should choose your friends, not let them choose you. He had so many so-called friends sponging off him when he was champion that they chewed into the vast fortune he made during his career. They were there in force to enjoy the good times. But where were they when the bad times came? When he was the champion defending his title he used to have as many as fifty or more people feeding off him like locusts, signing for their fares and hotel bills in his name. You will discover no hangers-on in the EastEnders stable. False friends are not welcome, thank you very much.

I got the feeling that Ali is now a lonely man. All the hangers-on have disappeared now that there's nothing left for them to grab. He deserved better because he was something very special, know what I mean?

While I was in Vegas I went out of my way to see the statue of my other great hero, Joe Louis. I was paying homage to a champion who represented his sport with great dignity and remains one of the most popular heroes in American sporting history. I visited the statue with Cornelius Boza-Edwards, the Ugandan-born former world junior lightweight champion who started his professional career in London before moving to Vegas to further his boxing ambitions in impressive style.

Louis was another like Ali who didn't enjoy the best of luck when his career was over. He was parted from his money by devious people, and ran up crippling tax bills that brought him to his knees when it was too late for him to earn any more money with his fists.

But something Louis never lost was the respect and admiration of millions of people around the world. His skill, punching power and his conduct both inside and out of the ring won him an army of fans, and when he died in 1981 a month short of his sixty-seventh birthday there was genuine sadness at the passing of one of the greatest and most loved sportsmen of the century.

I have studied Louis and Ali in action on my video for hours on end and can never make up my mind as to which of them was the better champion. Louis won sixty-eight of his seventy-one contests, most of them ending with a sudden explosive flash and with his opponents on their backs. His fists often didn't seem to move more than six inches, but the timing and follow-through was so perfect that his short, murderous hooks and crosses would suddenly turn strong, aggressive rivals to jelly.

Ali on the other hand rarely produced spectacular finishes to his contests. He won

The Joe Louis statue in Las Vegas. I went to pay homage to a great sportsman and the hero of millions. That's former world junior lightweight champion Cornelius Boza-Edwards with me. He is now based in Vegas but still looks on London as his home

fifty-six of his sixty-one professional fights and was noted more for the speed and accuracy of his punches than the power. He used to throw nearly all his shots to the head, whereas Louis could paralyse opponents with punches to the body as well.

The amazing thing about Ali is that he was out of action for those three and a half years in his mid-20s, which are reckoned to be the peak years for a heavyweight. He is the only heavyweight to have won the world title three times and during his twenty-year career became the best-known face - and voice - in the world.

Ali versus Louis, with both men at their peak, would be a dream fight and, to be honest, I struggle to pick a winner even after studying their fights so many times that I feel I know every move and punch. I've a feeling Ali would just nick it on points but who knows what would have happened if Louis could have pinned him with one of his devastating hooks to the jaw?

In my book, Ali and Louis are equal.

12: The Family Man

The most important people in my life are my girlfriend Laura and my beautiful three-year-old daughter Nicola. They are always at home waiting for me, and they quickly bring me down to earth and give me the sort of relaxation that is so vital when pressures are at their peak.

There are two Frank Brunos - the one the public sees who fights for a living, and then the private one who likes nothing better than to switch off and roll on the floor playing with his lovely baby girl. Nicola can do anything with me. I'm a real big softie from the moment she looks at me with her pretty eyes and gives me the sort of smile that would knock out any of my opponents far quicker than me.

She's a right chatterbox with a dozen questions always on the tip of her tongue. When I'm trying to creep out of the house in the early hours to start my training routine she often calls to me from her cot.

'Where are you going, daddy?' she asks.
'Running,' I say.
'Where?'
'In the woods.'
'Where are the woods?'
'Just a short drive away.'
'Can I come?'
'No, darling. Daddy has to run on his own.'
'Why?'
'Because I run fast.'
'How fast?'
'Very, very, very fast.'
'I can run fast.'
'Yes, darling. Now go back to sleep.'
'I want to come with you...'

By this time we will have woken Laura who takes Nicola into bed with her while I get on my way. They are precious moments that I wouldn't miss for the world.

Once the front door closes behind me I like our lives to be our own. I think everybody should be entitled to their privacy, and there have been several times when I've been made angry by reporters poking their noses in where they don't belong. The people I most admire in the whole world are Prince Charles and Princess Diana. I think we work Princess Di too hard, and I get angry when the press start raking up stories about her. How on earth she and Prince Charles can stand it I don't know. I get just a pinprick of publicity in comparison but there are some things that are written and said about me that really make me boil.

I don't want anybody writing or talking about my private life because it is nobody's business but mine. Laura and I plan to get married one day, but we will do it in our time and not be pressurized into it. It's not easy for Laura. She knows she has to take second place to my boxing. But she supports me all the way and spoils me at home by going out of her way to make me comfortable, relaxed and well fed. We've been together since the day we met at Battersea Park roller-skating rink when I was eighteen. She playfully pinched my behind as I was whizzing round the rink and that was the start of it all. We started seeing each other regularly and a strong love just sort of grew. I need the support and love that she gives me and I look on her as

The loves of my life. Laura and Nicola, whose smile would knock out any of my opponents far quicker than I could

This is how I like to have my hands full, with my lovely Nicola. There's no referee around to shout: "Stop holding, Bruno!"

somebody very special. Nobody can say she came after me for my money because when we met I had nothing but big ideas.

I've still got big ideas but am now much nearer being able to turn them into reality. I want to give Laura, Nicola and any other children God blesses us with a nice big home near the countryside, with a swimming pool and some stables so that

This is me being taken for a ride near Hyde Park. I first started riding while at Oak Hall Boarding School, and one day I would like to have stables and horses of my own

60

Laura, Nicola and I can go riding. Laura is, thank God, expecting our second child and if we're lucky enough to have a son I will teach him to play table tennis rather than box. I would want him to have a really good education and become a banker or a barrister, something like that. Not a boxer.

Boxing is a hard, hard business. You have to give it a hundred per cent and then some more. Laura comes to see me fight, but to be honest I shut her out of my mind. You have to wear blinkers going into the ring. The last thing any boxer wants near him on fight night is a nervous woman. Both Laura and I accepted right from the start of my career that we would both have to make sacrifices. There is plenty of time for the good life after I've hung up my gloves. I am determined not to make the mistake that Muhammad Ali and Joe Louis made and stay around too long.

I can't see myself being a boxer after the age of about twenty-eight. By then I hope to have got enough money together to live a comfortable life. There are some cranks out there who hate the thought of Laura and me making a go of it. The occasional nasty letter comes in among the hundreds of letters that I receive from genuine fans who have supported me all the way to my world championship fight. It's just stupid prejudice from people who know no better. They can't understand that Laura and I are among the majority of people who don't see black or white, only human beings. The good Lord created us all equal.

Just to discourage any cranks from paying us an unwelcome visit I keep my two Dobermans at home. Bomber and Angie are like members of our family and are marvellous companions. I walk - and sometimes run them - for miles. Both are gentle and loving, but I know they would quickly turn if anybody came to our house who was not welcome. I have had to put a printed note on my front door asking fans to kindly not ring asking for autographs. I am grateful for their interest and will go out of my way to give them any time I can spare when I am away from my home, but once the door closes behind me I need all the rest I can get.

Laura gets on marvellously with my family. Mum is naturally keen for us to get married and one day we'll give her that satisfaction. Not because the media are saying we should, but because we want to.

My family are important to me, particularly big brother Michael. He talks a lot of good sense and we spend a lot of time on the 'phone to each other swapping memories of when I was a real handful as a kid. We used to spar with each other at home in Wandsworth, but eventually there came a day when he realised he couldn't handle me any more. I suppose I was about fifteen and just beginning to feel my strength. Michael, a giant who looks down on me, remembers that suddenly I was moving him around as if he was a leaf in the autumn wind. That's how he recalls it.

It was Michael who was first to realise that I had been blessed with boxing skills above the normal. He used to watch me in my earliest days as an amateur and would say: 'Franklyn, you've got IT. God's spotlight has fallen on you. You are going to be a great, great boxer.'

This encouragement used to do wonders for my confidence and it was after I had won the London ABA heavyweight title when I was just eighteen that he wrote above the door in our kitchen: 'FRANK BRUNO, HEAVY- WEIGHT CHAMPION OF THE WORLD 1986.'

Michael and my sisters, Faye, Angela and Joanne, get behind me on fight night and their support means a lot to me.

I'm a lucky guy. I have the love of Laura and Nicola, the loyalty of my family and the encouragement and support of the Law-lesses, my second family.

So when you hear me saying after fights 'Thank God, 'Arry' you'll know that I am not just paying lip service. I really do have a lot to thank God for.

13: The Selling of Bruno

Almost as important as winning in the ring these days is selling yourself outside it. You have to turn yourself into a personality so that the public want to buy tickets to watch you, the press want to write about you, the sponsors want to be associated with you and the television chiefs want to turn their cameras on you. It means you have to be seen with the right people and in the right places. For the selling of Frank Bruno that meant a trip to Las Vegas where I could improve what is known in the business world as my media image.

I had just become the top contender for the world championship by beating Gerrie Coetzee in one round when it was decided that I needed to be 'seen around' in the United States where the boxing people with the big purse strings are based.

When Terry and I talk business together we always refer to Frank Bruno as if he is somebody else. Infact we call him just 'Bruno'. Terry says things like, 'I think this would be right for Bruno' or, 'I think this would be wrong for Bruno's image'. He never completes any business without consulting me first. I usually tell him: 'I'll leave it up to you.' Sometimes that annoys him. 'Listen,' he says, 'there will come a time when you are not boxing for a living and you will possibly become a businessman. The more interest you take now in business affairs the easier you will find it when you have to negotiate things for yourself.'

There was a load of nonsense written a couple of years back when the newspapers discovered that Terry had an interest in the promotions staged by Mike Barrett, Mickey Duff and boxing-fan businessman Jarvis Astaire. 'What d'you think of Terry Lawless being a member of the cartel?' reporters asked me. Cartel? I thought perhaps Terry had started a car renting business. 'Got a car, Tel?' That's me trying to be funny, know what I mean?

Anyway, Terry sat me down and explained everything to me and I quickly realised that his association with Barrett, Duff and Astaire was good news for me and all his boxers. He is the most honourable man I know and at no time, despite what was hinted in newspaper reports, did he put the interests of his boxers anything but first.

I just shrugged it off because to be honest I couldn't understand what all the fuss was about. Everywhere you look now there are managers who also promote and promoters who also manage. I could not see that Terry was doing anything that was worth a moment's concern.

It was Terry who suggested it would be a good idea for Bruno to be seen in Vegas immediately after the victory over Coetzee. 'Bruno is a big name in Britain,' he said, 'but we've also got to make it mean something in the States. That's where the big television money is, and the more they see of you over there the easier it will be for us to arrange a shot at the world title.'

The plan was for me to be at the ringside for the world middleweight championship clash between Marvin Hagler and John Mugabi. We knew that every top personality in the fight business would be there, along with dozens of world celebrities.

So for a week I stepped into the world of the superstars. I flew first class to Los Angeles - courtesy of the *Daily Mail* - and had hardly settled into my seat before the

The Strip at Las Vegas. All this could be mine if I were to win the heavyweight championship of the world, or so the publicity people told me. I think I'd prefer King's Road, Chelsea

introductions started. 'There's somebody here wants to meet you, Frank,' Terry said.

Instinctively, I reached into my pocket and took out a signed photograph of myself and put it into the outstretched hand of the person bending over me. I always carry a supply of the photos because (thank God) people are always asking for my autograph. When I looked up I found myself staring into the surprised face of pop superstar George Michael. It took George a few minutes to get over my gaffe in handing him an autographed picture, but then he sat down alongside me and we got talking about the pop world. If I hadn't gone into

boxing I would like to have had a go at singing for a living. My brother, Michael, is more musical than me and is a good keyboards player. I fancy myself singing in a Marvin Gaye or Stevie Wonder style.

Once we had got to Vegas the 'big sell' started. Photographer Monty Fresco and *Daily Mail* boxing correspondent Peter Moss saw to it that I met and was photographed with just about every major star in Vegas. First off, I was introduced to the glamorous Bo Derek. 'What are you hoping to do with your life, Frank?' she asked.

'I'm going to be the next world heavyweight champion,' I said.

She looked at me closely. 'Well you've certainly got the build for it,' she said. 'I wish you all the luck in the world, I really do.'

64

I was delighted to have met her but thought Dudley Moore was a bit generous with his ten-out-of-ten rating. More like an eight, I thought. She later asked pressmen: 'Who was that I was just photographed with?'

One day I hope she'll be proud to recall that she had her picture taken with Bruno.

Next I was introduced to Telly Savalas, who is a fight fan and had heard about my one-round victory over Gerrie Coetzee.

'That was some performance, baby,' he said, sounding as if he was using a Kojak script. 'Anybody who can do that to Coetzee has gotta be reckoned with. Who are you fighting next?'

'Possibly Tim Witherspoon,' I said.

He sucked in his breath. 'Gee, that'll be some fight,' he said. 'He's a mean fighter. You'll have to be real cool against him. Real cool.'

Ten out of ten if you recognise who this is with me. That's right, Dudley Moore's co-star in the film, 10, *Bo Derek*

Flying high with George Michael. I expected George to sing his No 1 hit, 'Different Corner'

It's like this, Tel....This is me giving Telly Savalas, better known as Kojak, the bare facts about boxing

I felt a shadow fall over me and looked up into the familiar face of Knight Rider star, David Hasselhoff. I couldn't believe how big he was. He towered over me at six feet seven inches.

He really knew his boxing. 'You're up there as a top contender after the way you saw off Coetzee,' he said. 'Witherspoon will be tough, but with your punching power there's nobody in the world who will feel happy having to fight you.'

When you're as big as Knight Rider David Hasselhoff you don't get any hassle, know what I mean?

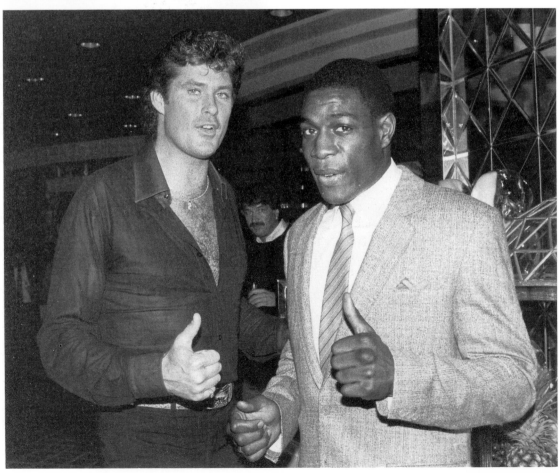

Here's my lovely second mum Sylvia Lawless, and that's her husband Terry and some geezer called Tom Selleck gatecrashing what was going to be a great picture of just the two of us.

I looked at him and wondered how he could handle himself. He was too pretty to have done any serious boxing. 'I like watching from the safe side of the ropes,' he said.

I don't want to pretend that I was becoming bosom pals with any of these stars. All these brief introductions were being made at an exclusive cocktail party at Caesar's Palace Hotel on the eve of the Hagler-Mugabi showdown, and to be honest I was not all that keen on the affair. In a way I suppose I should have felt overawed by it all because it was a billion miles away from the life I'd left behind at Wandsworth, but it all seemed a bit false to me. I went along with it because I knew the value of the publicity.

My next star appearance was alongside Tom Selleck of Magnum fame. He told me that he preferred basketball to boxing and had at one time considered a professional career after winning a basketball scholarship to the University of Southern California. He

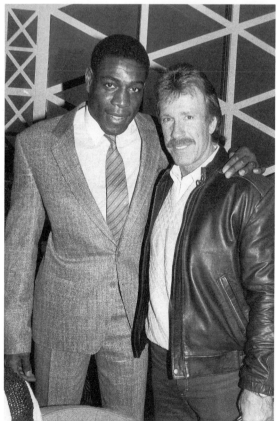

This man is chopping out a big career for himself in films....martial arts and screen star, Chuck Norris

A one-armed bandit could bring you this million-dollar jackpot in Vegas. But I will try to achieve it using two arms and, of course, two fists

reckoned that at six foot six inches tall he wasn't quite big enough to have made the grade in the American professional game!

I was also introduced to martial arts expert Chuck Norris and the giant Swede Dolph Lundgren, who had played the part of the Russian opponent in the latest Rocky film. I've seen all the Rocky films and have loved every second of them, but I reckon the way Sylvester Stallone fights on screen

he would last about two minutes against a top-flight heavyweight. Mind you, it might be different if he takes Rambo's gun into the ring with him!

The next day I was taken to one of the casinos and shown a well-guarded, glass-fronted display of one million dollars. There were 10,000 hundred-dollar bills to show the punters what they could win if they got

This is the only draw I've ever had in my career. I'm sure I am the first sheriff of the wild west to wear Nike trainers. The Nike shoes give a whole new meaning to 'running for sheriff'!

lucky on the jackpot. All I wanted to do was hit that jackpot in the ring. I was not in the slightest bit tempted by the gambling tables. I have to fight for my money and I ain't going to give it up easily, know what I mean?

It would be nice to win a million dollars with my fists. But a million pounds would be better.

Before going to the Hagler-Mugabi fight I went to a reconstruction of an old west town with Monty Fresco to pose for photographs as a cowboy. Anybody who saw Richard Pryor as the sheriff in *Blazing Saddles* should have a good idea how I looked.

Monty fixed me up with the cowboy gear but forgot to get a hat. A large American tourist came walking along the sidewalk towards us wearing the sort of ten-gallon hat that Monty wanted to give the final touch to his picture. Monty is as Cockney as they come and has a bit of a Donald Duck type of lisp. He stood in the path of the tourist and said: 'Excuse me, mate, I wonder if you'd let me borrow your hat for just a minute while I take a picture?'

The Yank looked down on a suddenly shrinking Monty and said: 'F--- off.'

'But this is Frank Bruno,' Monty said in desperation. 'He's the next heavyweight champion of the world.'

The Yank looked at me in my cowboy gear (along with Nike running shoes!) and shoved Monty out of his path. As he walked away from us he shouted over his shoulder: 'You're just a pair of f-----g panhandlers.'

Monty waited until he was out of earshot and then said: 'Some sheriff, you are. Why didn't you draw your gun and make him give us his titfer?'

I said: 'D'you know why I'm wearing these Nike running shoes, Monty?'

'Go on,' said Monty. 'Surprise me.'

'So I can run for sheriff,' I said. Monty didn't think it was funny either!

The selling of Bruno continued at the ringside on the night of the fight. I was introduced to two superstars of the screen, Burt Reynolds and Jack Nicholson.

'Nice to meet you, Frank,' Reynolds said. 'They tell me you could be the next heavyweight champ.'

'That's what I'm hoping,' I said, wondering if perhaps he could get Smokey and the Bandits to help me.

'We don't like the title going out of America,' he said, 'but good luck when you get the chance.'

Jack Nicholson peered at me through dark-tinted glasses. Just behind him stood a bodyguard who was nearly seven foot tall and as wide as a barndoor. I felt as if I was in a scene from *One Flew Over the Cuckoo's Nest*.

'How are you, feller?' asked Nicholson, obviously without a clue as to who I was.

'I'm fine, thank you Jack,' I said.

We posed for the photograph.

'Thanks, Jack,' I said.

'That's okay,' he said. 'Look after yourself now, you hear?'

And that was the selling of Bruno in Vegas.

I felt much more comfortable after the fight when I went to Marvin Hagler's victory party at Caesar's Palace. There I mixed with three of the modern greats of the ring, Hagler, Sugar Ray Leonard and Don Curry. I've got videos of all their greatest performances and I enjoyed talking boxing to them. All three of them had heard about my victory over Coetzee and were obviously impressed. At least I had the satisfaction of knowing that the people in the fight trade in America knew all about me.

When we arrived home Terry and I had an important business meeting about Bruno.

'I think Bruno has got to give up his European championship,' said Terry.

It was the only professional title I had won. I had taken it off enormous Swede Anders Eklund with a fourth-round knock-out victory at Wembley in 1985. It was my proudest possession.

'What's the problem?' I said.

Terry showed me a bulletin from the

Burt Reynolds was looking more than semi-tough at the ringside for the Hagler-Mugabi world title fight

European Boxing Union. 'You've been ordered to defend the championship against Dutchman Andre Van Den Oetelaar.'

'And that's a problem?'

'You'd have no problem beating him.' Terry said. 'He's not in your league. But you are so close to a world championship chance that it would be stupid to risk throwing it away'. He could just get lucky with a punch or you could get an injury and that would put our programme back a year. It's not as if you can earn big money with a defence against the Dutchman. He can't draw breath at the box office.'

I could see that Terry was agonising over me having to surrender the European championship.

I felt as if I was in a scene from One Flew Over the Cuckoo's Nest *when I joined Jack Nicholson and his man-mountain bodyguard at the ringside in Las Vegas*

'Terry, you're the boss,' I said. 'If you think I should let the title go then that's it. I'll go along with anything you say. Tell them they can have it back. At least I'll be able to say I was the undefeated heavyweight champion of Europe.'

So, without throwing a punch, Bruno was the ex-European champion. Now we had to step up the selling of Bruno for a world title fight against Tim Witherspoon.

14: Delivering the Punch Lines

I have been asked to do some pretty astonishing things since my boxing made me something of a public personality but Lenny Henry's request beat them all.

'Frank,' he said on the telephone, 'we'd like you to appear on the Comic Relief charity show at the Shaftesbury Theatre.'

'Great,' I said.

'You'll appear on stage with me.'

'Fine, Lenny. I look forward to it.'

'We're going to do the balcony scene from Romeo and Juliet.'

'Err...great. You did say Romeo and Juliet, Lenny?'

'That's right, Frank. And I'm going to play the part of Romeo.'

'I see, Lenny. And dare I ask what you want me to do?'

'Well we don't want you to play the part of the balcony, Frank. So that only leaves the part of Juliet.....Hello, Frank. Are you still there, Frank?

'You're not joking are you, Lenny.'

'No, Frank, I'm perfectly serious. It'll bring the house down. And maybe the balcony as well.'

And that was how I got roped into dressing up as Juliet and going on stage at the Shaftesbury Theatre. It was the most nerve-wracking and yet at the same time the most satisfying thing I have ever done outside the boxing ring. Let's be honest, I was not exactly familiar with Shakespeare. In fact as a kid I thought of Shakespeare ('The Shakespeare') as a South London pub.

What Lenny didn't tell me was that he was going to play Romeo while impersonating me. I've been a house guest of his and so he had plenty of opportunity to get my voice and mannerisms right. And he doesn't have to black up!

He sent me the script and I learnt it as best I could. We had just the one rehearsal and I was petrified about making a mess of it on the night. But as Lenny predicted, we brought the house down. That was mainly due to his brilliant take-off of me. It was so good that even I wasn't sure which of us was which.

We did three successive nights and every time I fluffed a line Lenny got me out of trouble with a brilliant adlib. On the first night we had planned for Terry Lawless to have a walk-on part. Lenny gave him his cue and we waited for his appearance but nothing happened. 'Wherefore art thou, Tel?' Lenny called out in a stage whisper. But still no sign of Terry, so we carried on with the rest of the sketch.

Later an embarrassed Terry had us in fits when he told us that he had got lost. 'I couldn't find the way on to the stage,' he said. 'I kept bumping into curtains and scenery. By the time I found the wings it was too late.'

Terry never loses his way to the ring, thank God. I don't know what I'd do without him in my corner.

I've been lucky enough to have been invited to make guest appearances with many of the funniest entertainers in the land and I am now experienced in front of the television cameras. I really enjoy the exposure and am not as tongue-tied as I used to be.

I remember that my first television appearance away from boxing was on Central Television with Jimmy Greaves. He was doing a series called 'The Greaves

Report' and he invited me up to Birmingham for a light-hearted interview. We did some sparring in a local gymnasium and that in itself was hilarious. I'm six inches taller than Jim and he was having trouble getting past my long arms to ask his questions. The plan was that Jimmy would 'fight' his way inside my reach and then interview me as he held on.

It was the idea of Gary Newbon, now the head of sport at Central. I don't think he quite appreciated the effort and energy you use even when sparring. Each time Jimmy fought his way close enough to ask his questions he was breathing like a winded bull.

He'd start the interview and the soundman would interrupt and say: 'All I can hear is heavy breathing.'

'You could sell the soundtrack for a bleedin' blue movie,' said Greavesie, with

That most impressive comedian Lenny Henry and I managed to make Romeo and Juliet more like Punch and Judy, But it was all in a good cause

that cutting tongue of his that has made him such a popular television personality.

After about six tries, Jim finally fixed it. 'I'll tell you what, Frank,' he said. 'You sit in the corner and I'll interview you there.'

A pity the cameras didn't follow us down the motorway when we left Birmingham, with Jimmy giving me a lift to London. We stopped off at a service station for a bite to eat and Jimmy had the place in uproar by going up to the biggest, toughest lorry drivers he could find and challenging them to a fight. Then he'd point at me and say: 'I should let you know that I'll be bringing on a sub.'

I don't think Jimmy has yet recovered from the fact that my food order filled three trays. And he was paying.

Freddie Starr has to be one of the funniest men I've ever met. I just can't keep a straight face when I'm anywhere near

Cannon and Ball had me doubled up when I appeared on their ITV show. The trouble with working with them is that you don't know what Bobby Ball is going to get up to next

him. You can be in the middle of a serious conversation when he'll suddenly make a rude noise and look at you as though you are the guilty party, then he'll mime blowing you a kiss and convince everybody looking on that you are a raving poufter.

He was a surprise guest when Eamonn Andrews trapped Terry Lawless with the 'This Is Your Life' Book. The morning of the show I told Terry that I was going for a massage but slipped away for a filming session with Freddie. He did a brilliant take-off of Muhammad Ali when sparring with me, including the Ali Shuffle and all Ali's fancy footwork. But every time I stuck out my left jab he would take it on the nose and go into an exaggerated stagger.

Then he looked into the camera and said: 'Terry, all these years you've been bandaging your fighters' hands wrong. This is how you should do it.'

He took out a huge roll of bandage and started to wind it round my hands in the orthodox way. Then he started to wrap it round my arms and up and around my shoulders. By the time he had finished I was wrapped in bandage from head to toe like an Egyptian mummy. You've heard of Big Daddy. Well, Freddie had turned me into Big Mummy. When it was shown on television the camera was speeded up to make it even funnier.

My first comedy appearance on BBCtv was with Les Dawson. Reg Gutteridge, ITV's boxing commentator and one of the most knowledgeable men in the business, took part in a boxing comedy sketch in which I had to knock Les out. To give Les his punchline I had to say after knocking him down: 'I've got good news and I've got bad news...' Suddenly I had the nightmare of what they call in the business 'drying'. My mind went a complete blank and I couldn't remember what I had to say. Reg sensed that I was struggling and fed me beautifully by saying: 'I hear you've got some news for us...?' That got my memory working and I said: 'Yeah, good news and bad news...' Les, lying flat out with his

This is a hold up! I had my hands full with Little and Large when I appeared on their BBC comedy show

eyes closed, opened one eye and a smile crossed that lovely craggy face of his as he realised what was going on. Thanks to Reg's quick thinking we got through the sketch without having to do a re-take.

Cannon and Ball are among my favourites and I've done a couple of shows with them. The trouble with working with them is that you never know what Bobby Ball is going to get up to next. I find I'm so busy laughing at him that I forget to deliver my punchlines at the right time.

I have also been on shows with Jim Davidson, Little and Large, Cilla Black and

Here's a bundle of laughs - Norman Wisdom, a former Army flyweight boxing champion who is a regular ringside fan on big fight nights

Eamonn Andrews, a real boxing buff who was kind enough to invite me to make two guest appearances on his What's My Line? show. The panel knocked me out very quickly each time. I spent the day at the races with Terry Wogan when he was hosting the Derby Day show from Epsom for BBC Radio's 'Sport-on-Two' and I couldn't help marvelling at his way with words. He was having all sorts of technical problems but nothing put him out of his stride.

Two of the biggest boxing fans among the celebrities are Frank Carson and Norman Wisdom. I've had the pleasure of

mixing socially with both of them and I've been really impressed by their knowledge of the fight game. Norman Wisdom, for me one of the funniest men on earth, used to be an Army flyweight champion and goes out of his way to be at the ringside for the big fights.

Many of the comedians I've mentioned have looked in to see me in my dressing-room before I go into the ring. It's great of them to take the trouble, although they don't find me a particularly good audience. In the last hour before any contest I like to pour all my concentration into the job ahead. It's being single-minded that has helped me get where I am in a business where one loss of concentration can wreck your career.

The entertainer who has helped me most is Terry's pal Roy Castle. He has given me tap-dancing lessons to help me loosen up and improve my balance and rhythm. I get breathless watching Roy dance and I'm not surprised that his marathon tap-dancing sessions have brought him a place in the *Guinness Book of Records*. His close interest in my career is greatly appreciated.

While I'm name-dropping I shouldn't forget to mention Prince Philip, who I was privileged to meet at a Royal Variety Club function. He impressed me as a man who clearly knows a lot about all sports.

You are no doubt sick to death of me mentioning all the people.I've met, but the Frank Bruno story wouldn't be complete if I didn't paint a picture of how a poor, undisciplined black kid from Wandsworth has managed to find a respected place in society.

And it's all thanks to boxing. Those well-meaning but interfering people who

A Wogan winner. Terry Wogan and I help Gloria Honeyford aboard the Sport-on-Two bus at the Epsom Derby. Terry is not just all talk. I really admired the way he coped with presenting his programme despite all sorts of technical difficulties. A great pro. I wish he'd spare me a few of his words, know what I mean?

*I have tapped Roy Castle for tips on balance and
rhythm. Roy's tap dancing has earned him a place
in the Guinness Book of Records*

Here I am with a real live Prince and two kings of the boxing ring. Floyd Patterson, Charlie Magri, and I were privileged to meet Prince Philip at a Royal Variety Club function

would have the sport banned should bear in mind that there are dozens of others like me who would have been lost on the scrapheap but for boxing. It brings discipline and, most important of all, *hope* into our lives. I would rather take the risk of getting hit on the head by a gloved fist than face a future without a job, without pride and without hope.

Now instead of looking at Frank Bruno on the scrapheap I can invite you to look at me in my scrap album, a collection of pictures of my fights and thoughts on the way up the boxing ladder to a challenge for the greatest prize in sport - the world heavyweight championship.....

The sweetness of victory as captured by Observer photographer Eamonn McCabe. Terry Lawless and Jimmy Tibbs are what you might call as pleased as punch as I do a Nureyev after beating Anders Eklund for the European title. I would like to thank all the writers and cameramen who have helped me relive my career on the following pages of my Scrap Album....

FIGHT No. 1
Opponent: **Lupe Guerra (Mexico)**
Venue: **Royal Albert Hall**
Date: **17 March, 1982**

My knees were wobbling before my professional debut against Lupe Guerra. It was getting on for two years since I had last climbed into the ring, and during my lay-off I had been to Bogota for the eye operation and had got myself involved in a lot of hassle over who was to manage me.

I had Terry alongside me, thank God, to keep my nerves under control as I walked from the dressing-room to the Albert Hall ring. There was a lot of pressure on me because I had been given a big build-up in the press. I wasn't worried about the fight but very anxious not to let people down. I knew a lot was expected of me and it made me nervous.

I had seen my opponent at the weigh-in. He had a worn face that looked as if it had been on the end of a lot of punches. He was shorter than me by about three inches and when he first saw me walk stripped to the scales I could see a sudden flicker of doubt in his eyes, know what I mean? It's not for me to boast about my physique but I have always been well built and I know that when opponents get a first glance at me they are often, as Terry puts it, 'unnerved'.

I shook Guerra's hand just before going onto the scales, and he gave me a half smile that changed into a snarl as he seemed to remember that I was the man he would be fighting a few hours later. Terry has always impressed on me the importance of appearing confident and self-assured at weigh-ins. It is a vital part of the psychological warfare. I try not to be cocky and flash but make sure I ooze confidence. I weighed in at just half a pound under fifteen and a half stone and had a twenty-one pounds weight advantage.

'Nice and cool, Frank,' Terry said as I waited for the first bell of my professional career. 'Open him up with your jab and just take your time. Be lucky.' As the timekeeper shouted 'seconds out' all my nerves disappeared and I felt in complete control of myself. This was the moment I had been dreaming about for years. Frank Bruno, professional boxer.

Suddenly I was out into the centre of the ring, jabbing like Terry had told me. Guerra came at me aggressively and got through my defence with a couple of quick left leads of his own before coming in close and holding my right arm in a vice-like grip.

Referee Paddy Sower pushed us apart, and I was astonished to find that Guerra had switched from an orthodox stance to southpaw. Barely a minute of the fight had gone and already he was trying old pro tricks that were new to me.

I managed to connect with my first combination, a left-right to the head, and I felt him wobble. He grabbed my gloves and I had to wrestle him off me. His legs were shaky and he stumbled to the canvas. I went to a neutral corner and watched Guerra scrambling on his hands and knees as the referee counted over him. I looked to my own corner where Terry was miming a left lead.

Guerra got up at eight and came towards me with his head down. I turned the left jab that Terry was advising into an uppercut and he dropped back to the canvas. After another eight count, the unhappy-looking Mexican got up and shaped to throw a desperate haymaker as I walked in behind a long left jab. I felt the power surging through my body as I let rip with the sort of

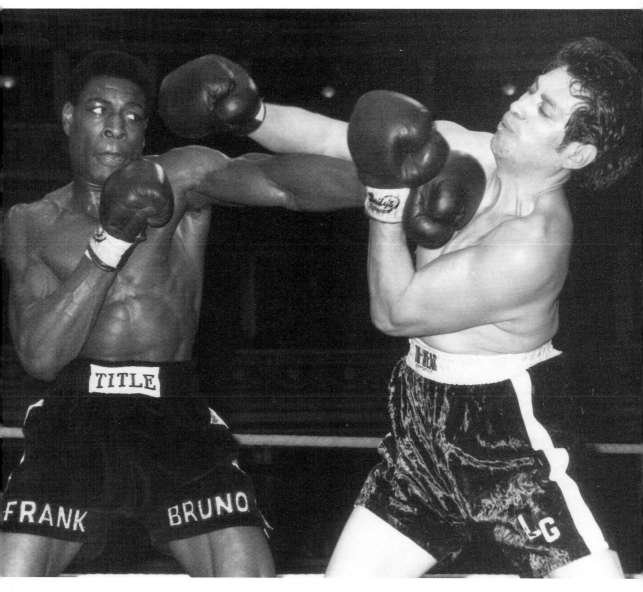

Crafty Lupe Guerra tried to confuse me in my professional debut by switching to a southpaw stance, but I still managed to get the measure of him with my left jab

four-punch combination to the head that I had been learning in the gym. They all landed on target, and Guerra fell backwards to the canvas and I knew that this time he wasn't going to beat the count. It was all over with just under half a minute of the round to go.

'We have lift-off!' said Terry as I returned to the corner after helping Guerra to his feet. 'Just listen to the reaction of the crowd. They loved it.'

I looked down to see ringsiders on their feet applauding. It was one of the most satisfying moments of my life. Frank Bruno was on his way.

FIGHT No. 2
Opponent: **Harvey Steichen (USA)**
Venue: **Wembley Arena**
Date: **30 March, 1982**

For my second fight I returned to Wembley Arena almost two years to the day since I had won the ABA heavyweight championship there in 1980. My opponent was Harvey Steichen, a stocky, barrel-chested American from Carson City. He talked a good fight at the weigh-in. 'You're gonna be in big trouble tonight, Bruno,' he said as he tipped the scales at a couple of pounds over sixteen stone. I was going to have to give away nearly a stone, but I noticed that he had a lot of surplus weight around his waist and I knew just from looking at him that he was not a fitness fanatic like me.

'He can be a dangerous brawler,' Terry told me. 'Take it easy in the first round and get a good look at him. Keep that left jab in his face.'

I did exactly as Terry told me and kept my left jabs queueing on the end of Steichen's broad nose. He was an unconventional fighter who threw wild, swinging punches from odd angles. I just kept stepping inside them and banging my left in as straight and as hard as I could. By the end of the first round I noticed that Steichen was beginning to breathe heavily and his face had gone a pinky red colour from where my left fist was landing.

As I returned to the corner Terry gave me a pat on the shoulder as he sat me down. 'Just right, Frank,' he said. 'You've sickened him with that left jab and he's already running out of gas. You can try some combinations in this round and fire your right over the top of his left. He leaves himself wide open every time he throws it.'

Steichen swung an out-of-range left early in the second round and I saw the chance to cross with my right. It landed with a downward chopping effect on the side of his head, and as he staggered sideways I followed up with a left hook that dropped him onto his knees in my own corner.

He got up at five and came swinging at me wildly. I threw four successive rights, none of which connected with full force but the power was enough to send him falling face first to the canvas. Referee Harry Gibbs counted to nine, and as Steichen got up he cuddled both arms around him and led him to his corner. I had won the scheduled eight rounder with thirty seconds of the second round to go.

'You've got a good one here, Terry,' Harry Gibbs said as he came to my corner and raised my hand. 'You can go a long way in this game, son, provided you look after yourself.'

They were encouraging words coming from the man acknowledged as Britain's number one referee.

A happy night for me was scarred when my stablemate Maurice Hope failed to regain the European light-middleweight championship. Most people thought Mo had done enough to win on points against Italian Luigi Michillo, but he lost it on a split decision. Typically of true sportsman Mo there was not a murmur of protest, and he announced that he was retiring at the end of a marvellous career during which he had become the first black immigrant boxer to win a world championship for Britain.

Terry told me: 'If you can approach boxing and life with the same dignity and dedication as Mo then you will have done yourself proud.'

That's exactly the way I felt.

I managed to get a peep at another

heavyweight contest on the bill in which former British heavyweight champion Gordon Ferris narrowly outpointed a useful-looking New Yorker called Barry Funches over ten rounds. I wondered how long it would be before I was boxing in their class.

I made full use of my height and reach advantage against stocky Harvey Steichen. He was a dangerous brawler but did me the favour of continually running into my left glove

FIGHT No. 3
Opponent: Tom Stevenson (USA)
Venue: Royal Albert Hall
Date: 20 April, 1982

I got my first taste of a crowd booing one of my contests and I didn't like it one bit. On paper my third opponent, Tom Stevenson, from Indianapolis, looked a good test for me. He had won eleven of his twelve professional contests in the United States and had a reputation for being a devastating knockout puncher.

Terry had done his homework talking to his many contacts in America, and he had found out that Stevenson is what is known in the fight trade as a good 'on top' boxer. That is if you allowed him to dictate a contest he could be dangerous.

'You've got to assert your authority right from the first bell,' Terry ordered. 'Don't let him settle. Keep him on his back foot and don't let him set himself for counter punches. Hands high all the time and make that jab really count. Don't paw with it. Punch with it.'

I really got myself keyed up for the fight because I thought I was in for a hard night's work. At 14 stone 8 pounds Stevenson was giving me ten pounds and at the weigh-in he looked to have a good build on him and appeared to have all the confidence in the world. 'I haven't come all this way to lose,' he told reporters. 'I've never heard of this guy Bruno but he's sure going to know all about me.'

All I found out about him was that he seemed not to want to fight. He hid behind a high guard and hardly threw a punch as I stalked him, wondering what tactical plan he was trying. He stabbed out a couple of tentative lefts that fell short, and when I rammed home three stiff jabs to the head his eyes opened wide as if to say: 'Hell, if this is his left jab what's his right like?'

He soon found out. I threw a long right hook that landed high up on his temple. Stevenson retreated back to the ropes as I followed up with a full-blooded left-right combination that landed on his gloves which he had cupped to his face. The force of my punches lifted him backwards and through the middle rope onto the ring apron.

There were jeers and boos from the crowd as Stevenson sat on the ring apron, making little effort to get back through the ropes as referee Larry O'Connell counted him out.

Some of the boos were directed at me as if it was my fault Stevenson had not put up more resistance. The British Boxing Board of Control announced that they were suspending Stevenson's $1000 purse pending an investigation.

I felt as frustrated as the fans, but must say in Stevenson's defence that those punches of mine that hit his gloves were meant to knock holes in him. The power was enough to put him through the ropes and I think they knocked all ambition and heart out of him. 'I was overawed by the occasion,' Stevenson said later. 'Bruno caught me with some really heavy punches and when I went through the ropes I got confused. That guy can really punch.'

'Take no notice of the boos,' Terry told me. 'They're not used to you yet. It will take them time to realise that every one of your punches is a heart-breaker.'

I found it hard to sleep when I got home that night because I had so much unused energy. I was up early the next morning and out on the road running, and it was seven or eight miles before I felt I had run my frustration off.

There were already digs coming from some quarters claiming that I was being fed

The only title I want is the world heavyweight championship. Know what I mean, 'Arry?

My first triumph at Wembley - victory in the 1980 ABA final against Welshman Rudi Pika. I was just eighteen and the youngest ever winner of the title. It was after this contest that I got together with champion maker Terry Lawless

Just seconds to go to my world title eliminator against Gerrie Coetzee and Terry Lawless takes a final, meaningful look

Mr and Mrs Lawless proudly parade their world champions - Mo Hope (at the front) and Jim Watt, John H. Stracey, and the clowning Charlie Magri. I am the odd man out at this gathering because I have not won a world title. Yet!

The loneliness of the long distance runner. I am up with the birds every morning and usually cover seven miles

I love getting my skates on. When I say I'm getting the rollers out people think I've really struck it rich

Ta ta, Tom. My third opponent, Tom Stevenson, disappears through the ropes and if you look closely at this picture you will see that the only way I was in danger was from his right boot. Ouch!

easy touches. And this was after just *three* professional fights following my long lay-off.

Eric Armit, a renowned boxing statistician, boosted my confidence when he told Terry: 'Frank deserves praise not criticism for his performances to date. I've been looking into my records and find that Guerra had won seventeen of his twenty-three fights before fighting Frank. So that was a tough debut for him. Harvey Steichen had gone the distance with John Tate and had been stopped just six times in thirty-three fights. Stevenson's only defeat in eleven contests was on a cut eye, and he had scored six first-round wins.'

Terry passed these facts and figures on to me and I felt a whole lot better. Despite what some critics were saying, I had beaten three opponents who could not be dismissed as bums.

FIGHT No. 4
Opponent: **Ron Gibbs (USA)**
Venue: **Wembley Arena**
Date: **4 May, 1982**

For three rounds I struggled to get into my rhythm against Ron Gibbs, a slippery opponent from Nevada. He was the classiest fighter I had met to date and he frustrated me by clever use of the ring. My left jab wasn't landing with its usual power and accuracy, and he was parrying and then shooting over fast right counters.

If you're wondering how I've got such good recall of the action from each of my fights it's because - thanks to the BBC - I have a video collection of all my professional contests and I watch them for hours on end to analyse myself and figure out where I can improve and sharpen my punch combinations and my all-round ring strategy.

I look back now at those first three rounds against Gibbs and I'm almost embarrassed. I can't believe that I used to be so stiff and tense. Terry told me at the end of round three: 'You've got to loosen up, Frank. You're trying too hard. Relax and just let your punches go naturally. You'll eat this feller if you just pick your spots. He's made for your left hook. Try hooking off the jab because he gets careless and drops his right.'

It was me who got careless early in the fourth round and Gibbs startled me with an uppercut that clipped me on the chin. He then dropped his right ready for another crack and I let a left hook go with a full pivot of my shoulder and hips, turning my wrist to get a corkscrew effect at the moment of impact.

This was as good a punch as I had ever thrown and Gibbs fell sideways into the ropes as if I had hit him with a hammer. I thought it would be the last punch I would need to produce that evening because I felt the impact of it all the way up to my elbow. But Gibbs astonished me by just managing to beat the count. It proved he must have a chin like granite.

He was badly dazed and a sitting target for my punches. I was relieved that referee Roland Dakin moved in to save Gibbs as I measured him for my big bombs.

The Wembley crowd gave me a great ovation, and I think that one left hook had convinced many of them that perhaps I was a genuine prospect after all despite the stick some of the critics were giving me over the choice of opponents.

Gibbs told reporters: 'That was one helluva left hook he caught me with, but until then I was not impressed. We've got guys back home in the States who would walk right through him.'

I knew that Gibbs hadn't seen me at anything like my best. I was developing a bad habit of pawing with my left jab, and until I produced the left hook the timing on my combinations was nothing like as sharp as I needed it to be.

But at least I had proved I could take out a fair-class opponent with just one shot. That did wonders for my confidence.

In a post-fight press interview, Terry said: 'I think all you pressmen are forgetting that Frank is still raw and inexperienced. His entire amateur career covered less than sixty rounds and he has yet to complete eight rounds in total as a professional. You all appear to think he should be the finished

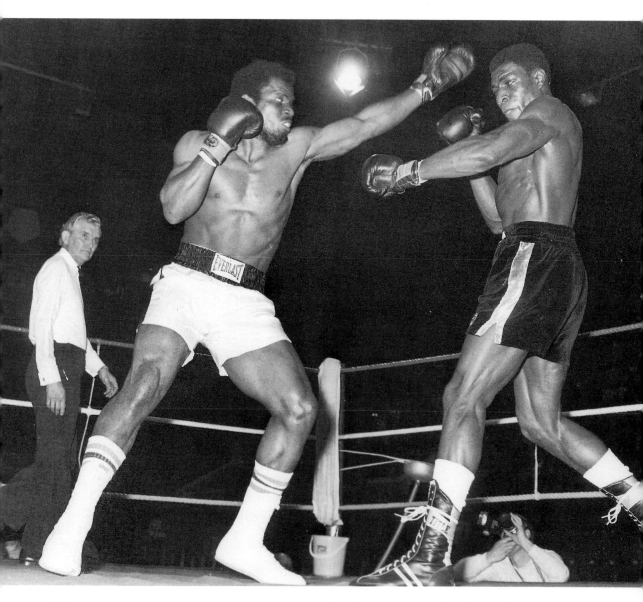

Ron Gibbs swings into the attack but is way off target. Terry Lawless told me: "He's made for your left hook." And, as usual, Terry was proved right

article. It's going to be three or four years before you see the best of this feller. Just be patient.'

Three or four years? I thought of the prediction that my brother Michael had written on the kitchen door at home: 'FRANK BRUNO, HEAVYWEIGHT CHAMPION OF THE WORLD 1986.' But I didn't mention anything to the press boys. I didn't want them to think I was being flash, know what I mean?

FIGHT No. 5
Opponent: **Tony Moore (GB)**
Venue: **Royal Albert Hall**
Date: **1 June, 1982**

Tony Moore was a have-gloves-will-travel fighter. He had journeyed all over the world from his Hendon, Middlesex, base taking on some of the best heavyweights around. While I was having my fifth fight he was coming up for his fifty-fourth. Tony, who I knew and liked, was convinced that I was making a major mistake taking him on.

He couldn't forget that I had sparred with him during my amateur days, and still thought of me as that baby he used to mess around in the gym. But the baby had grown up!

Tony is a nice feller but gave me quite a bit of verbal punishment before the fight. He didn't seem to think I deserved the publicity build-up that I was getting and made no secret of the fact that he was going to put me in my place.

He was a wise old pro and I realised that the things he was saying were meant to make me jittery, but I just turned a deaf ear to them and worked extra hard in training. He was my first domestic opponent and I knew the media would watch the fight closely because they were going to be able to measure me against a fighter whose form and record they knew.

Tony had lost twenty-four of his contests but was noted for being an iron man of the ring who usually managed to go the distance. Terry was half hoping that Tony would show his durability against me. 'You need the experience of going at least six or seven rounds,' he said. 'All these quick finishes are impressive but what we want is an opponent who can stand up to your punches. I think Tony could be just the

I am about to stand and deliver against Tony Moore, a fighter of vast experience who surprised me by continually backing on to the ropes. Tony decided to quit boxing after I had stopped him in two rounds

man.'

Sorry, Tel, but Tony wasn't the man. He semed to lose his heart for the fight within the first minute, after I had softened him up with a few full-power left jabs that I threw with all my shoulderweight behind. He became very apprehensive and tried to smother and hold rather than let his own punches go.

I was surprised that a man of Tony's vast experience should keep going back onto the ropes where he was an easy target for my punches. Maybe he was trying to lure me onto one of his favourite left hooks. If he was, his plan failed miserably.

When the bell ended the first round I had already given him a good tanking by trapping him on the ropes. As I walked back to my corner I knew, without being flash, that he was not going to give me the distance experience that I needed.

At 15 stone 5 pounds I had a weight advantage of just over a stone, and I made full use of it in the second round. I forced him back and unleashed a long left-right-left combination that I had been practising in the gym. It was a left jab, right cross and left hook - all thrown with maximum power and each punch landing to the head.

Poor old Tony went down like a sack of potatoes, not knowing whether it was Christmas or Easter. He bravely dragged himself up at nine but fell back against the ropes, and as I moved forward to complete my night's work referee Sid Nathan jumped in between us to save Tony from a bigger hiding.

Back in the dressing-room Tony announced that he was hanging up his gloves. He'd had a long, 12-year career and with better guidance might have gone right to the top. I wished him a long and happy retirement.He deserved it.

FIGHT No. 6
Opponent: **George Scott (GB)**
Venue: **Wembley Arena**
Date: **14 September, 1982**

During the summer of 1982 Terry took me on my first learning trip to the United States. I went to work, not to play. I trained and sparred in gymnasiums in New York, Los Angeles and Las Vegas and really got the flavour of the big fight game in America. My stablemates Mark Kaylor and Tony Adams were with me, and all three of us picked up lots of tips that helped improve our boxing ability.

Most memorable for me was working out in California with Mike Weaver, who was then the reigning WBA champion. He had won the title late in his career at the age of twenty-seven and told me: 'Frank, you're a baby yet and have all the time in the world. Don't rush things. You've got everything going for you. Don't throw it away by being impatient.' We had a great sparring session and Mike paid me a lot of nice compliments. He was a sincere, genuine person and I was grateful to him for taking so much time and trouble to help me.

I also had some useful training sessions in the 42nd Street gym in New York that was bursting at the seams with hungry fighters chasing their dreams. There were a lot of very heavy people around, and I'm not talking about weight. That's a rough, tough world out there and you've really got to be on your toes and thinking ahead of the rest to survive. Whoever first called New York a concrete jungle got it exactly right.

You need eyes in the back of your head when you're walking through those tough New York streets. I went out on my own for a stroll down 42nd Street one afternoon and bumped into Johnny Boss, a well-known American boxing agent.

'Who's with you?' he asked, looking around to see who was accompanying me.

'Nobody,' I said. 'I'm just taking a stroll on my own.'

'Are you mad or somethin'?' he said. 'You may be a big guy but that won't frighten the muggers off. For God's sake get back to your hotel and don't come out on your own.'

My stroll became a trot as I hurried back to the safety of the hotel where Terry was waiting for me and looking anxious.

'What's the matter?' I said.

'I've just had Johnny Boss on the 'phone,' he said. 'He was worried about you. John said that gold necklace and watch you're wearing make you a target for the muggers. When you go out in future take a cab.'

New York? Give me London any day.

I was busting to get back into serious action when I returned from the States and looked forward to trying out all that I had learned against George Scott, the former Northern Area heavyweight champion from Newcastle who had a reputation for being strong and durable.

At the weigh-in I scaled my heaviest-ever 15 stone 8 pounds, but I was still having to give a couple of pounds to Scott who also had a slight height and reach advantage. He was known as the 'King of Geordieland', and during the build-up to the fight had promised to end my unbeaten run.

George Scott, the uncrowned king of Geordieland, looks ready to bow out of our short-lived contest. He did not have the satisfaction of landing a single punch

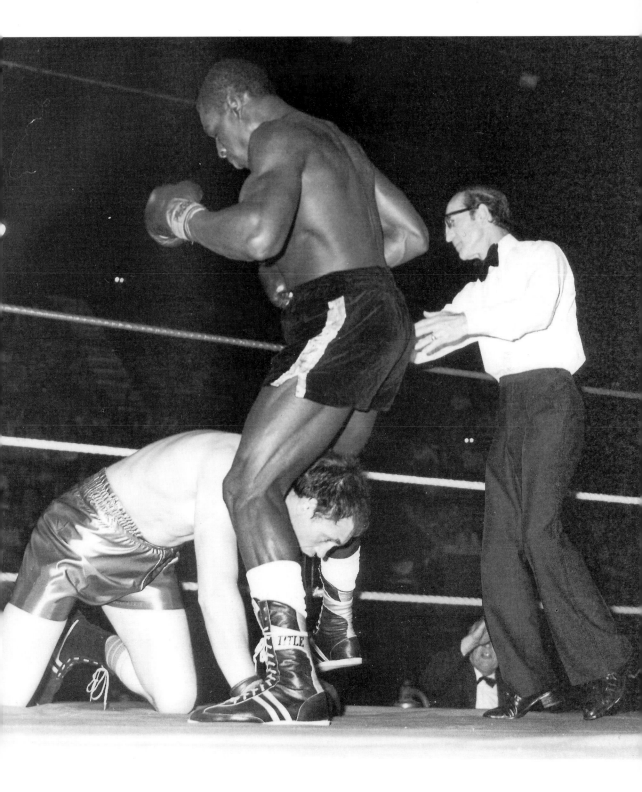

Never in my life have I slagged off an opponent and I'm not going to start now. I have too much respect for anybody who has the courage to climb through the ropes. But I feel that Scott must know in his heart that he let himself down against me. It was all over in the first round and I can't recollect him hitting me with a single punch.

He seemed to lose interest from the moment I threw an uppercut through the middle of his defence and jolted his head back. The punch landed as I drove him towards my own corner, and he sagged to the canvas and took an eight count.

I could sense that he was already a beaten man. He had a hunted look in his eyes but in the ring there's no place to hide. Scott retreated to the ropes and I practised my combinations. Solid, straight left, then a follow-through right, a left uppercut, right cross and finally a full-power left hook that sent him back to the canvas.

He made it obvious that he had taken enough when he got up at eight. As I moved forward he ducked his head and hid behind his gloves. It left referee Sid Nathan with no alternative but to stop the fight. There were loud boos from the fans, but they were aimed at Scott who had failed to live up to all his promises.

There was already talk about me being a contender for the British championship, but Terry told me to ignore the reports. 'You're still wearing "L" plates,' he said. 'I want to get the pressure off you while you're developing. I think we'll take a fight abroad out of the spotlight.'

FIGHT No. 7
Opponent: **Ali Lukusa (Zaire)**
Venue: **West Berlin Sportshalle**
Date: **23 October, 1982**

There are losers and there are losers. I reckon poor Ali Lukusa was just about the unluckiest of all the fighters I have ever met. I'm not talking so much about our fight as about what happened to him afterwards.

Terry has good contacts throughout the world of boxing, and he took me to Berlin to box because he wanted to relieve the

I knocked out Ali Lukusa in two rounds in Berlin and I think Terry was fairly pleased with my performance

enormous pressure that had been building up at home. He was concerned at the way people were expecting mature performances from me even though my entire professional career to date had lasted less than twelve rounds. He also felt that fighting abroad would be valuable experience for when I had to fight at top international level.

The Berlin promoters came up with what on paper looked to be a demanding examination for me. Ali Lukusa was born in Zaire and boxed out of Spain where he was

reckoned to be a heavyweight of championship class. He had a very respectable record and was said to be as strong as an ox.

I got a great welcome in Berlin, and I found the fans to be very knowledgeable about boxing. They had not had a decent heavyweight in Germany since the retirement of former European champion Karl Mildenberger and were keen to see big men in action.

Terry suggested a cautious start against Lukusa. 'Tuck up and get behind your jab,' he said. 'Stay on top of him but don't take chances until you've seen what he has to offer.' That was my fight plan, but it went out of the window when I made Lukusa wobble with the first serious punch that I threw.

I thought to myself: 'Aye, aye, Frank, this feller ain't going to be around long.'

He was taller than me and quite a bit heavier and he tried dancing out of range in a sort of Ali style, but I cut off his escape route by trapping him in a corner. I ripped in two left hooks to the body and a right to the head that had him down for a nine count. I watched him carefully when he got up because that's when opponents can be at their most dangerous, just like wounded lions.

There was vicious intent in his eyes and he let a volley of punches go, but I tucked up like Terry had told me and blocked them on my elbows. I quickly regained control, and threw an overarm right that stopped him in his tracks and sent him sprawling to the canvas. He was up at nine, and just as I was about to move in the bell rang to save him from what I intended to be a finishing punch.

When Terry gets excited he has a habit of shrugging his shoulder as if he's slipping punches. The old shoulder was working overtime when I returned to the corner. 'That was perfection, Frank,' he said. 'You've laid the foundation. Now go out and finish the job. You can't miss him with your right.'

Laid the foundation? I preferred this sort of foundation work to slaving on a building site.

Lukusa came out for the second round with his hands held high, and tried to stop me setting myself for an attack by getting close to me. I let him come to me and then buried a left hook just above the waistband on his shorts and brought an uppercut sweeping from hip level. It hit him right on the point of the jaw and he fell at my feet as if he had been shot. The ten-second count was a formality.

There were no boos from the ringsiders and the Berliners stood and cheered me. My first experience of fighting overseas could not have gone better.

But it had been a bad night for Lukusa. And worse was to come. He went for a walk outside his hotel later that evening and got beaten up in the street by what he said were four British soldiers.

He was glad to see the back of Berlin and of Bruno.

FIGHT No. 8
Opponent: **Rudi Gauwe (Belgium)**
Venue: **Royal Albert Hall**
Date: **9 November, 1982**

I had trained to meet Austrian Helmut Owessle, but he pulled out and a much tougher opponent, Rudi Gauwe, came in as a late substitute. The Belgian had fought at the Albert Hall in 1980 when John L. Gardner, then a member of Terry's 'EastEnders' stable, forced him to retire after nine rounds of a fight for the vacant European championship.

He was the most experienced of all my opponents to date, and everybody seemed convinced that he would make me work hard and get some much-needed rounds under my belt.

At 15 stone 6 pounds I had a four-pound weight advantage, and I noticed at the weigh-in that Gauwe looked a bit thick

Rudi Gauwe feels the full weight of the left jab that had been sharpened and improved at the Royal Oak gymnasium under the watchful eye of trainer Jimmy Tibbs

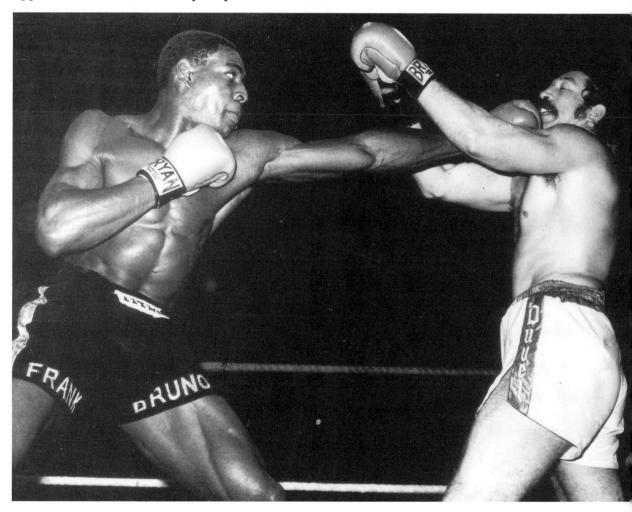

around the waist. My trainer Jimmy Tibbs advised an early bombardment to the body, and throughout the first round I concentrated on jabbing to the head and then sinking hooks in underneath with both hands. Each time I landed Gauwe grunted like a winded pig and he was puffing and panting at the bell.

My self-confidence was getting stronger all the time, and looking back at the video of the fight it's interesting to see that I was much more relaxed and loose-limbed than in my early contests when I was too stiff and upright. I noticed on the video that Gauwe threw several dangerous rights that I slipped inside almost casually or blocked with my glove. I was at last producing my gymnasium form in the ring.

The first punch of the second round, a stiff left jab, thumped against Gauwe's nose and split the bridge. I then followed on with an overarm right to the side of the jaw and he fell backwards with his right leg twisting under him.

He was grimacing with pain as referee Sid Nathan counted him out, and when he finally got up he limped heavily back to his corner. The crowd booed him but I think the spectators would have been more sympathetic had they realised he had broken an ankle when he went down.

Joe Bugner, who had just started a comeback campaign, was sitting at the ringside with promoter Frank Warren. As 'Fanks 'Arry' Carpenter was interviewing me in the ring Joe kept holding up an open hand to signal that he would beat me in five rounds. I mimed that I could take him out in two.

But there was no chance of Terry letting me fight Joe for at least six months. 'There are two reasons,' he explained. 'One, the longer we keep him waiting the bigger the interest and the purse will be. Two, you need a lot more experience. Joe knows all the tricks and could mess you around. I *think* you could beat him now. I *know* you will beat him in six months' time. Let him wait. You have all the time in the world.'

FIGHT No. 9
Opponent: Georg Butzbach (West Germany)
Venue: Wembley Arena
Date: 23 November, 1982

I had been working really hard at improving my punches to the body with trainer Jimmy Tibbs in the Royal Oak gymnasium. It's the big punches to the jaw that get the spectators excited but a good shot to the body can be just as effective. I proved exactly that against Georg Butzbach, a blond, long-haired West German who looked to me to have an inviting stomach.

Butzbach, who weighed five and a half pounds less than me at 15 stone exactly, rushed out at me as the first bell rang and was obviously looking for a quick finish. I made sure he got it!

I stayed cool as Butzbach threw a lot of wild leather. His punches were whizzing past my head and I satisfied myself with picking him off with long left leads. He kept up his two-fisted attack, but there was no accuracy in his punches and I was slipping and parrying them and just biding my time.

The first round was two minutes old when I saw my chance. Butzbach came charging forward with his elbows out, something we are taught not to do in the 'EastEnders' stable. I arched to my left and sent a left corkscrewing into the pit of his stomach. The German yelled out with pain and sank to the canvas as I threw a following right that swept through his mop of blond hair.

He took a count of seven on one knee and was obviously struggling to catch his breath. The punch had knocked all of the wind out of him and when he got up he turned his back on me and raised an arm in

Georg Butzbach squats in pain while I acknowledge the cheers (and some boos) of the Wembley fans. My left to the pit of the German's stomach made him cry out in agony

surrender. Referee Roland Dakin stepped in between us and it went down into the record books as a first-round retirement.

There were some boos from the spectators at the back of the arena but those close to the ringside appreciated just how devastating my left to the stomach had been. It was as good a body punch as I had ever thrown and was a sure sign that all my hard training was paying dividends.

Terry was delighted with my performance against an experienced opponent whose record suggested he could take a punch. But all the gloss was knocked off my victory the next day when British Boxing Board of Control secretary Ray Clarke was quoted as saying: 'The honeymoon is over. Bruno must now meet men with more experience and of more substance.'

I have rarely seen Terry as angry as he was over this statement. He told Colin Hart, of the *Sun:* 'I respect Ray Clarke. In fact I am one of his greatest admirers because of the tremendous job he does for our sport. But I'm certainly not going to allow anyone else to manage Frank Bruno.

'Frank has beaten his nine opponents inside the distance and all of them were thoroughly vetted by the Board. It is not our fault that they become so intimidated by Bruno that they refuse to fight on the night.

'If the Board try to make me put him in with men that I consider are over his head we will pack our bags and go to the States. There he can get the experience he needs without the inquests after every fight.

'This country has been crying out for a world heavyweight champion since the beginning of the century. Now we have suddenly found a boy who might make it one day we should be bending over backwards to protect him as much as possible.'

Terry wasn't bluffing. He was determined not to rush me to the top and I will always be grateful to him for pacing my career exactly right. To be honest, I felt I could have been fighting better-known opponents, but I now know that Terry was a hundred per cent right to keep a tight rein on my career. I was still at the learning stage.

FIGHT No. 10
Opponent: **Gilberto Acuna (Puerto Rica)**
Venue: **Royal Albert Hall**
Date: **7 December, 1982**

It was a British Boxing Board of Control official who recommended Gilberto Acuna as a suitable opponent for my tenth fight. He had won twelve of his twenty professional contests and had lasted six rounds against Joe Bugner in Los Angeles in 1980.

He lasted just forty seconds against me. I threw a light left lead and then a measured right cross to the side of the head and he crashed backwards to the canvas. Acuna

My fastest victory. Gilberto Acuna is on his way down and out in just forty seconds. He beat the count but was in no fit state to continue when he got up on rubber legs

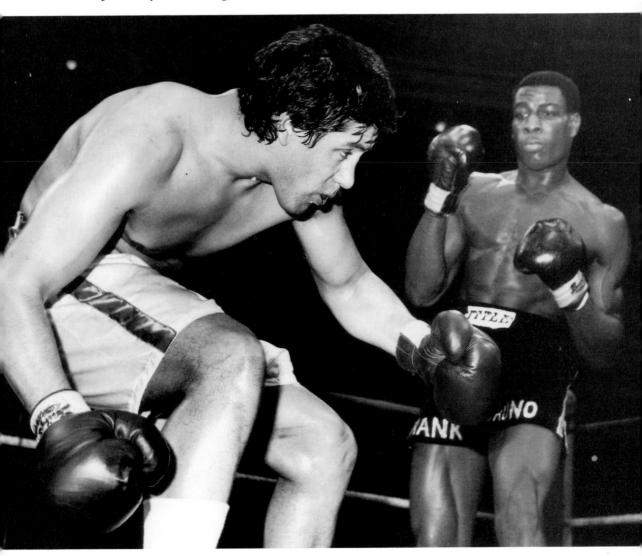

was up at five, but his legs were shaking as if they were made of jelly and referee Harry Gibbs signalled to me that he had seen enough and raised my hand in victory.

Board of Control secretary Ray Clarke told Neil Allen of the London *Standard* after the quickest win of my career that he was 'not altogether happy' about the match, yet the Board had given the contest their blessing after one of their stewards had seen Acuna knock out Eddie Cooper at Walthamstow.

There was a lot of booing from the fans who obviously felt that Acuna could have carried on, but believe me he was in no fit state to defend himself. I have had the power of my right-hand punch tested by scientists who reported that when I'm letting it go at full power it travels at twenty miles an hour and lands with a force of half a ton.

It was travelling at top speed when I connected with Acuna's face. If it had connected just an inch or two lower I am sure he would have gone down for the full count. As it was the punch scattered his senses and when he got up his legs betrayed him with a sort of delayed impact effect.

About this time they were making a lot of fuss about another heavyweight prospect called Funso Banjo, a London-based Nigerian. His manager Jimmy Quill pointed out that he used Acuna as a sparring partner and made no secret of the fact that he thought Banjo could box my ears off.

Banjo made his Albert Hall debut on the same night that I beat Acuna, and was slow-handclapped by the fans as he struggled to an eight-rounds points victory over Mick Chmilowsky of Edmonton.

Terry never gets involved in slanging matches, but I wanted to shout from the rooftops that I could have beaten Banjo with one hand tied behind my back.

I looked forward to a nice pay day against him but the fight never materialised, mainly because his negative style of boxing just wasn't attractive enough. I never go round mouthing off about other boxers but I really had to bite my tongue over Banjo because his followers were saying some nasty, hurtful things about me.

One thing the boxing business has taught me is to grow a second skin. I have learnt to ignore what people say about me and my performances. All I know is that I have to satisfy myself.

I was satisfied that I had done a thoroughly professional job against Acuna and that's all that really mattered to me.

That was my boxing programme for 1982 finished. Ten fights, ten inside-the-distance wins and they had lasted less than seventeen rounds in total. All in all, it had been a year to remember.

I couldn't wait for the New Year when I felt I could start establishing myself as a genuine contender in the title stakes.

FIGHT No. 11
Opponent: **Stewart Lithgo (GB)**
Venue: **Royal Albert Hall**
Date: **18 January, 1983**

Stewart Lithgo put a lot of spice into the build-up for my first fight of 1983. He was convinced I had been fed a diet of pushovers and made no secret of the fact that he was going to give me a good hiding.

Lithgo, a former jump jockey who had outgrown his sport, was the twenty-five-year-old Northern Area champion from Hartlepool. Since turning professional in 1979 he had won fourteen fights, drawn one and lost three. He was unbeaten in his first thirteen fights and earned himself a place in a British championship eliminator against Gordon Ferris who hammered him to defeat in two rounds.

He now saw the chance of re-establishing himself as a title contender by knocking me out of his path. Lithgo wasn't exactly short of confidence. He told John Jarrett in the trade paper *Boxing News:* 'I don't think Bruno is anything special at all. He hasn't fought anybody yet. In fact he hasn't even been hit. He's been knocking over selling platers. The wife could have knocked out the last two mugs he met. Bruno may have been billed as the great British hope but I intend to knock him down to size.'

His manager, Dennie Mancini, added: 'Bruno is finally going to meet somebody who will fight back. Stewart knows that this fight, especially if he wins, will make him into a hero.'

What Lithgo didn't know is that I almost had to pull out of the fight because of a really bad cold. It affected me when I was running and sparring and so I didn't get the hundred per cent preparation for the fight that I like. In fact I caught the cold off one of my sparring partners who went down with 'flu in the middle of my training programme. Terry and I discussed pulling out, but I started to pep up a few days before the contest and decided I could go ahead.

I expected to have a staring match with Lithgo at the weigh-in, but he was delayed on the train south from Hartlepool and so I didn't see him until we climbed into the Albert Hall ring. When he took off his dressing-gown I couldn't believe what a beanpole build he had. He was as tall as me but only scaled just over 13 stone 10 pounds and was the lightest of all my opponents.

There was no love lost between us after all the nasty things that he had said, and I went out with the intention of beating him in style. But I found him a really awkward cuss to fight and I gave what I reckon was the most unimpressive performance of my career.

I've got to give Lithgo full credit. He fought as if his life depended on it, and there were times when he put me under a lot of pressure with long, swinging punches that didn't hurt me but made me cover up and protect myself behind a high guard. I found the range with my left jab after a quiet opening round and made his nose bleed with four good stiff jabs. This would have knocked the heart out of many fighters, but Lithgo gritted his teeth and launched a two-fisted attack that had me defending myself for the longest spell since I had turned professional.

I thought I had put his lights out early in the third round when I caught him with a nicely timed right cross. His lanky frame shook as if he was suddenly standing on moving ground, but instead of falling over he came swarming all over me with his arms going like windmill sails.

'You've got a hard nut here, Frank,' I

Stewart Lithgo was an awkward opponent who fought as if his life depended on it. The former jump jockey was the first fighter not to fall against me

told myself as I looked out at him from behind the protective shield of my gloves.

About halfway through the round I threw a right hook that opened a nasty gash on Lithgo's cheekbone, just below the left eye. Then I made him grunt with a left hook to the body and a right uppercut to the chin. He took a backward step and came back fighting, and we were standing toe to toe swapping punches when the bell rang to end the round.

Terry gave me a rollocking when I returned to my corner. 'Don't get involved with him, Frank,' he said. 'He's gradually coming apart but you're giving him hope by standing and mixing it with him. Dictate with your left and pick your moments to throw your right hand over the top. Don't take any silly chances.'

I boxed more coolly in the fourth round and kept Lithgo on the end of my jab. Several of my right hooks thudded against the cut on his cheekbone and I could see that it was now spreading up and around his left eye. A lot of the strength had drained from his punches but he was still dangerous and keen to have a go.

As the bell ended the fourth round I sensed that I was not far away from victory. But it came quicker than I expected because his corner retired him after referee Sid Nathan had been called over to inspect the deep cut by his eye.

It was a wise decision although Lithgo didn't think so. He was furious when Dennie Mancini retired him, and I thought that for a moment he was going to start another fight in his own corner. Speaking selfishly I would have liked to have had one more round because I am convinced I could have knocked him down. He was the first opponent never to have taken a count against me and so I suppose that was a victory of some sort for him.

I normally exchange some friendly words with my opponents at the end of a fight but Lithgo didn't want to know. 'You're still nothing,' he snarled.

I shrugged and returned to the dressing-room where I told the press that while Lithgo was the gamest fighter I had met he had not managed to hurt me once. The fact that I didn't have a mark on me supported what I was saying. I could have told them about how bad my cold had been but I didn't want anybody to think I was making excuses.

When I got home I went into a deep depression because I knew I had not performed at anything like my best. I played the fight over in my mind as I lay in bed and thought of all the combinations I could and should have used against Lithgo.

I was up at five the next morning and out running, but I still had difficulty breathing because of my heavy head cold. After a relaxing sauna I met up with Terry and told him about my breathing problem. He arranged a hospital X-ray for me and the doctor told me there was nothing wrong that a few days' rest from training wouldn't cure. But I took no notice of him. You get work-aholics. Well I had become a sort of train-aholic. Terry realised this and gave me a good talking to. 'You are working so hard that you are leaving a lot of your form in the gym,' he said. 'Don't be quite so intense with your training. Relax more. Your career is coming along exactly as planned. I couldn't be happier with you. Just ease up a little on your training and I promise you will get the benefit in the ring.'

I took Terry's advice and lifted my foot off the accelerator. Just a little. And it made all the difference. Terry told the press: 'I have had to give Frank a telling-off for training too hard.'

But it was still better than slaving on the building site.

FIGHT No. 12
Opponent: **Peter Mulendwa (Uganda)**
Venue: **Royal Albert Hall**
Date: **8 February, 1983**

I was as excited as a little kid being shown what he was getting for his birthday present when Terry told me who was lined up as an opponent for my first top-of-the-bill contest. 'We've got you Alfredo Evangelista,' he said. 'It will be a ten-rounds international contest and it will be the mainline fight at the Albert Hall.'

Evangelista! The former European champion would give me a real step-up in class. The Uruguyan-born Spaniard had made two challenges for the world heavyweight title, going the distance with Muhammad Ali and getting knocked out in seven rounds by Larry Holmes.

I collected every fight video of Evangelista in action that I could lay my hands on and studied him for hours until I felt I knew his style almost as well as I knew my own. It looked to me as if his weak spot was his body. I noticed that in several fights he really winced if ever an opponent dug a punch into his stomach.

Trainer Jimmy Tibbs encouraged me to sharpen my combination punches to the body. We spent hours in the Royal Oak ring while he held the coaching pads at around waist height, circling away from me and calling out in rhythm as I let hooks go with both hands: 'One, two, three, four. And again. One, two, three, four. Take that Evangelista. And that. One, two, three, four....'

With less than a week to go to the fight I was in the best condition of my life. I had

This left uppercut had been meant for Alfredo Evangelista but it was poor Peter Mulendwa who was on the receiving end. I felt sorry for Mulendwa and I helped him back to his corner after I had knocked him out

109

taken Terry's advice and was making sure I relaxed more away from the gym. The thought of fighting Evangelista had given me the biggest boost of my career so far, and I was wound up ready to produce my best performance. So you can imagine how deflated I felt when on the Sunday before the Tuesday fight Terry rang me to say: 'Sorry, Frank, but Evangelista is out. He broke a wrist while training yesterday.'

I was choked. 'So what happens now?' I said.

'We've found a substitute who was in training for another fight,' he said. 'It's Peter Mulendwa, a Ugandan who is based in Italy.'

Mulendwa. I had just about heard of him but he meant nothing in world boxing, not like Evangelista.

When we met at the weigh-in I couldn't believe how small he looked. He weighed the same as Stewart Lithgo (13 stone 10 pounds) but was nowhere near as tall, and to me he seemed more like a light-heavyweight. When he saw me strip off I think he wondered how on earth he had allowed himself to be talked into taking this late-notice job.

I'll be honest, I really felt sorry for him. And that's the last way you should feel before climbing into the ring for a ten-round top-of-the-bill contest.

Terry sensed how I was feeling. 'You have got to get it into your head, Frank, that Mulendwa is a dangerous opponent,' he said. 'All right, he's not Evangelista. But you have got to convince yourself that he is just as big a threat to you and all your dreams and ambitions. You've got to pump yourself up for a thoroughly professional performance.'

I managed to bury the sympathy I felt for Mulendwa once we were in the ring, and I concentrated on softening him up with long, straight lefts for two rounds. He kept boring in at me, ducking low and protecting himself behind a high guard. The Ugandan was looking to land with roundhouse rights, but he was telegraphing the punches and I was able to comfortably block them or step inside and let them whiz harmlessly round the back of my head.

In the third round I stepped up the pace and the power of my punches and I could sense him running out of steam. Suddenly, midway through the round, I unleashed one of the body punches I had been saving for Evangelista. It was a right hook and Mulendwa gasped as I sunk it deep beneath his ribs.

He tried to fall forward into a clinch but I backed away ready to toss in some head punches. He tried but couldn't hide the effect of the body shot, and he suddenly reeled away from me and sprawled in his own corner clutching his stomach.

Referee Harry Gibbs counted the sorry-looking Mulendwa out and then I went and helped him up and back to his cornerstool. All my sympathy was back and I felt like weeping for him. He just did not belong in the same ring as me. I hope that doesn't sound flash. It's just fact.

There were boos from spectators who thought Mulendwa had gone down without taking a punch. But it was delayed reaction to a body shot that I know would have knocked the wind out of a bull.

I just wish it had been Evangelista who had been on the receiving end.

FIGHT No. 13
Opponent: **Winston Allen (GB)**
Venue: **Royal Albert Hall**
Date: **1 March, 1983**

Joe Bugner's comeback had pumped new interest into the heavyweight division and the air was thick with talk of a long-awaited Bruno-Bugner showdown. Much of the talk was being done by Joe's outspoken Australian wife, Marlene. Joe would have been world champion if he could have fought half as aggressively as she talked.

I was ready to fight Joe. Any time, any place. But Terry was still preaching the virtue of patience. There was also a political wall between Joe and me. He was in the camp of Frank Warren, who had lately arrived on the scene as a rival to the long-established Mike Barrett-Mickey Duff team.

I have to admit that Bugner was bugging me. He was one of the best defensive boxers in the world, no question of that. He had twice gone the distance with Ali, had outpointed Henry Cooper, had given Joe Frazier a hard time in a distance fight and was noted for the toughness of his chin. But he was also one of the most boring of all heavyweights to watch because his style was so negative. I would have jumped at the chance to test Joe's chin with my right hand, but I had to make do with trying to show that anything he could do I could do better.

It took him six rounds to beat Gilberto Acuna. I managed it in forty seconds. In his comeback campaign he had stopped Winston Allen in three rounds after looking in a bit of bother and stopped Eddie Neilson on cuts in five rounds. Now it was my turn to take on Allen, and if I could beat him then southpaw Neilson was next in line.

Allen, a black Welshman from Swansea, was reckoned to be one of the hardest hitting heavyweights around. He had used his flashing right fist to score one-round knockout victories over Stan McDermott and former European champion Jean-Pierre Coopmans, and he had shown durability in going the distance with powerful punchers David Pearce and Alfredo Evangelista.

I made a careful video study of Allen and was concerned at the dangerous way he used his head. He often butted like a billy goat, and Joe Bugner complained about his tactics during their fight and also claimed that Allen had at one stage bitten him.

I've heard of hungry fighters but that's ridiculous!

Allen said a lot of insulting things about me before the fight that gave me an extra incentive to put him in his place. I don't mind boxers making outrageous statements to help sell tickets, but he was digging in with comments designed to get under my skin and really hurt me. He succeeded and now I wanted to get my own back in the only place where it really mattered - the ring.

The fight was staged on St David's Day, and Terry said that the only leeks Welshman Allen had were in his defence.

Before the fight there had been a lot of discussion in the media as to whether or not I could take a punch to the chin. I had not, thank God, been tested in that department and Allen was reputedly the hardest puncher I had met to date. What would happen if he bounced his big right hand against my chin?

The answer came within less than a minute of the opening round. Allen threw a looping right that landed flush on my jaw. It felt as if I'd had an electric shock and I took a step backwards. I didn't want to let Allen know that he had hurt me and I quickly came back with a couple of hard straight lefts. But what I was saying to myself was: 'Blimey, Frank, you don't want to take any

Joe Bugner, whose comeback had livened up the heavyweight division. I would have jumped at the chance to test Joe's chin

more of them. Keep on red alert and get this feller out of the way at the first opportunity.'

It took me about ten seconds to get my senses together and then I really started to punish him. Jab, jab, jab, jab into his face and then thumping rights into his ribs as he tried holding me to stop the leather pouring into his face. I was more tense than I like to be in a fight, but Allen was made for my

straight left and he was almost eating it. At one stage he ran all the way along one side of the ring in an effort to avoid it but I kept after him. He tried in desperation to throw another one of those looping rights, but this time I covered up and it had lost its sting by the time it reached the side of my head.

I don't think I had ever felt so mean in a fight. Allen had really got me riled up and I wanted to hurt him. Left jab, left hook and then a right cross. All the punches were thudding home and I knew he was in big, big trouble. He hung on at every opportunity and referee James Brimmell briefly stopped the action while he warned Allen to stop holding.

Terry was looking concerned when I returned to the corner. I think that right hand had shaken him more than me. 'Are you all right?' he asked.

'Yeah, I've got him in my sights,' I said, feeling really confident.

'Just don't take any silly chances,' Terry warned. 'He's always going to be dangerous with that right. Your jab is working like a dream. Let your combinations go in this round. Every time he throws his right he drops his left. He's made for your right hook or right cross.'

Predictably, Allen threw that right of his as he came out at the start of the second. He might just as well have sent me a postcard to say it was coming. I stepped inside it and powered two stiff left jabs in and then two clubbing rights to the side of his head. Then I tried a short right hook that hit him high on the temple and he stumbled sideways. Just as Terry had warned, though, he was still dangerous with that right and he attempted a counter that missed the target but made me be a little more cautious. I knew it was only a matter of time now before he caved in under the pressure that I was applying, and I wasn't going to give him even half a chance to get back into the fight.

A left cross pulled him upright in his tracks and then I followed on with a heavy right that shook him from head to toe. He

The end is in sight for Winston Allen as I jolt him with a left cross. My right is ready for launching on to his unprotected jaw

was now standing still and I could sense that all the resistance was draining out of him. I was getting ready to unload my biggest bombs when he suddenly turned his back on me, spitting his gumshield out as if to signal that his evening's work was over. It was a total surrender and referee James Brimmell wrestled me away and raised my hand in victory before I could let any more punches go.

To add to my satisfaction I had beaten Allen in quicker time and more impressively than Joe Bugner. And I had proved that I could take a punch (which was one test that I would have preferred to have avoided, know what I mean?).

It's part of the fight business not to like your opponent in the ring and I certainly didn't like Winston Allen that night. But I later accepted that he had not really meant all the nasty things he had said about me, and he has since helped me out with sparring and the bad feeling before our fight is now forgotten history.

FIGHT No 14
Opponent: **Eddie Neilson (GB)**
Venue: **Royal Albert Hall**
Date: **5 April, 1983**

Like Joe Bugner, Eddie Neilson has a wife who can talk a good fight. She gave me a lot of verbal hammer before her husband and I finally settled our differences in the Albert Hall ring. An interesting fight would have been Mrs Bugner versus Mrs Neilson!

Of all my fights to date, this one caused Terry most sleepless nights. Neilson, a West Country fighter from Swindon, was my first southpaw opponent and he was reckoned to be one of the hardest punching heavyweights in Europe - a bigger hitter and a better all-round fighter than Winston Allen.

He had been more than holding his own against Joe Bugner until he was stopped with cuts in five rounds. His punching power was undisputed, but there were question marks about his defence and I was confident I could crack it open.

It's traditional for a right-hand punch to be favoured against a southpaw by an orthodox fighter, but in training Jimmy Tibbs worked on sharpening my left hook as well as my right. He knew that it could be just as effective against a 'wrong-way-round' opponent. I worked out against two southpaw sparring partners and practised throwing left hooks followed by right crosses. I watched a video of Neilson's fight against Joe Bugner and stored it in my memory that he liked to fight out of a crouch, so I knew I would be best advised making full use of my reach advantage and also that uppercuts could pay dividends if he came at me with his head-down, bulldozing tactics.

Mr and Mrs Neilson had made a lot of noise about how Eddie was going to use me

I am halfway through the left hook-right cross combination that gave Eddie Neilson double trouble. He was as brave as a lion but I was ready for Eddie

as a punchbag. They had gone on record as saying they were willing to back their confidence with a £1000 sidestake bet, but I noticed nothing was mentioned about the money when we came face to face at the weigh-in. Eddie weighed in at 15 stone 9 pounds and was just one and a half pounds heavier than me.

It seemed Neilson had brought half the West Country with him to the Albert Hall and he got a tremendous reception when he climbed into the ring. His wife and young son were at the ringside and I silently wished they had stayed away because I knew there was no way Eddie could beat me.

I had trained for a hard battle but found it a surprisingly easy night's work. I'll say this for Eddie, he was as brave as a lion and didn't let himself or his supporters down. Anybody with less courage would not have come out for the second round after I had given him a terrible hammering in the first three minutes. I could hear his little boy shouting from the ringside: 'Come on, Daddy.' The professional in me made me shut this out of my mind. You daren't be soft and emotional in the ring.

In the opening seconds of the contest I landed with the left-right combination to the head that I had been practising in the gym. They were not full-blooded blows but there was enough power behind them to topple Eddie to the canvas.

He was up quicker than was wise for him and I went after him with all guns blazing. He tried to come in close as I rocked him with punches from long range. I met him with short hooks and uppercuts and he was back on the canvas, this time for a count of eight.

Eddie ducked low and came charging at me with a brave counterattack, but there was none of his feared power in the blows and I rocked him back on his heels with a volley of lefts and rights. As I mounted what I meant to be a final attack he touched down on one knee for a count of two. It was a shrewd thing to do because it made me briefly lose my momentum. As he went

back to his corner at the end of the round he had a slight trickle of blood coming from the region of his right eye.

It was one of the most action-packed first rounds I had ever been involved in and Terry told me to cool down. 'The only hope he's got now is to pin you with one of his big punches,' he said. 'So he is going to be going all out early in this next round. Just be ultra careful, keep your hands up nice and high and pick your spots.'

I was content to box my way through the second round, dictating the fight from the middle of the ring behind a left jab as Neilson came at me bobbing and weaving and trying to land the big bombs that had brought him a string of inside-the-distance victories.

He caught me with a couple of good body shots but they didn't bother me in the slightest. I replied with a right under his heart, and I could see by the look on his face that the punch briefly took his breath away.

I had deliberately slowed down the pace in the second round and had held back on my heaviest blows, but when I went out for the third I intended to let Eddie feel the full weight of my punches. He came bulldozing at me, and as I moved back towards the ropes I fired a looping right hook that travelled in a wide arc before landing with a loud whacking sound just above his right eye.

He went down to the canvas with a thump and screwed up his face with pain as he knelt on his knees listening to referee Sid Nathan's count. Suddenly blood spurted from above his right eye where the punch had landed, and when Mr Nathan realised how badly Eddie was cut he immediately stopped the fight without continuing the count.

Neilson's disappointed fans shouted some insulting remarks at me on my way back to the dressing-room, but it didn't bother me. I know that I had proved myself the guv'nor and once again I had won in quicker time and much more convincingly than Bugner.

FIGHT No. 15
Opponent: **Scott LeDoux (USA)**
Venue: **Wembley Arena**
Date: **3 May, 1983**

Scott LeDoux, a brawler from Minnesota, had been in with the very best heavyweights around. He held both Ken Norton and Leon Spinks to draws, was narrowly outpointed over twelve rounds by Mike Weaver and went seven rounds with Larry Holmes in a 1980 challenge for the WBC crown. As far as Mr LeDoux was concerned I was a nobody, and he tried to put the frighteners on me.

When we met at the weigh-in on the afternoon of the fight he took me on one side and said: 'Here, boy, this is for you.'

He stuck a picture in my hand of a boxer with a battered face. 'That, boy, is my last opponent and that's how he looked after I'd finished with him. You'll be getting the same treatment tonight, boy.'

I thought for a minute I was out in the cotton fields. It was a real master and slave scene. The way he called me 'boy' really got under my skin, and Terry could see I was ready to blow my top. 'Take no notice of him, Frank,' he said. 'He's an old pro and is just trying to wind you up. Save it for the ring. Then you can show him just what a big, strong boy you are.'

LeDoux's attitude surprised me. It was hardly the sort of behaviour you would expect from a man who earned his living away from the ring as a schoolteacher.

During the build-up to the fight, former world heavyweight champion Floyd Patterson had spent some time in the Royal Oak gymnasium showing the value of getting my shoulder behind the jab. I got the feeling that Floyd was not that impressed by me when he watched me sparring, but he had become a 'Bruno believer' by the time he had witnessed my fight with LeDoux from a ringside seat at Wembley.

I had watched LeDoux on video against Greg Page and was encouraged by what I saw. He was a square-on, walk-in fighter who liked to throw swinging punches from a crouching position. I reckoned he was made to measure for my left jab.

LeDoux weighed in at 16 stone 2 pounds and had a six-and-a-half-pounds weight advantage. He didn't look built for speed, and so I went out with the intention of setting a fast pace. I found it easy to pick him off with the jab as he retreated with a crab-like style, suddenly launching counter-attacks that were, to be honest, surprisingly crude for a fighter of his vast experience. I noticed that he carried his left hand recklessly low and was a sitting target for a right, but I deliberately held back. 'Save that for later, Frank,' I told myself. 'Sicken him with the left for the time being.'

I knew I was having success with my jabbing methods because his face started to puff up and looked a blotchy red where my glove was thumping home. He was dangerous with swinging, two-fisted lunges but they were telegraphed and I found it easy to block them. After pouring in a procession of left jabs I threw one of my favourite combinations that trainer Jimmy Tibbs had helped me perfect - a left hook off the jab. When you throw a hook immediately after a jab it comes in from out of your opponent's line of vision. LeDoux had no idea what had hit him and sat down on the canvas with a bump. He was up at five, but the look in his eyes told me that he was already wishing he was back home in Minnesota.

LeDoux came out for the second round like an angry bull. He was trying to bully me out of my stride and was swinging long rights that were putting ringside spectators in more danger than me. I met him with solid left jabs flush on the nose, and his attempted rally slowly ran out of steam. Then I started to bring my right hand into

Scott LeDoux reluctantly takes a seat in the first round after I had clumped him with a left hook. He was kind enough to rate me one of the world's top five punchers

the argument and I jolted his head back with heavy overarm rights.

He bulled his way past my jab, and tried to rough me up at close quarters, using his head as a third glove. Referee Larry O'Connell was quick to spot him trying to butt me and warned him to be careful. I found a better way to warn him. I whacked him with a right hook that landed just above his left eye and split the eyebrow.

LeDoux was experienced enough to know he was now fighting on borrowed time. He started the third round with a desperate two-fisted attack, and managed to get through my defence with a left hook that acted as a warning to me not to get careless. I went back to my first-round policy of throwing plenty of heavy left jabs and blood started to pour from the injured eye as LeDoux's head was continually jolted back. About halfway through the round Larry O'Connell stopped the fight and called for a towel. He wiped the blood from LeDoux's face and after inspecting the damage signalled that it was all over.

LeDoux, so unpleasant before the fight, was suddenly sweetness itself. He put an arm around my shoulders and told me: 'You've got what it takes, Frank. I just couldn't get past that jab of yours. I've been in with the biggest punchers and you can match any of them. Be lucky now, you hear?'

Floyd Patterson came into the dressing-room and congratulated me. 'That was a very mature performance, Frank,' he said. 'Your jab was just beautiful. You made LeDoux eat it. Just be patient and one day you will be right there at the top.'

That coming from a man who had been to the top - winning the world title twice during his career - gave my confidence another vital boost. And I promise you that confidence is the most important of all hidden weapons in boxing.

FIGHT No 16
Opponent: **Barry Funches (USA)**
Venue: **Royal Albert Hall**
Date: **31 May, 1983**

I had been mentally preparing myself for a showdown with Joe Bugner, but boxing politics had killed off any chances of us getting together for a big pay day as well as a big punch up. I am convinced I had the power to beat Bugner, but I concede that he was an expert defensive boxer who could have posed me a lot of problems before I managed to get through with my bombing combinations.

It would have been just the experience I needed at that stage of my career, but it wasn't to be and so I had to clear my mind of him and think ahead to my next opponent - Barry Funches, a punching postman from New York who had featured on the Wembley bill against former British champion Gordon Ferris when I made my second appearance as a professional

Some of the critics were dismissing Funches as 'strictly an opponent' whose record was punctuated with defeats. But they were not having to climb into the ring with him, and I approached the fight with my usual total single-mindedness and concentration.

Like any of my opponents, Funches deserved my full respect. He had outpointed a good-class opponent in Mike Koranicki, and in his previous fight had given a rising American prospect called Eddie Gregg a lot of trouble before getting stopped in the eighth round. He may, on paper, have looked a pushover to some people but there is no such thing as a pushover in the ring.

When you're on a winning streak in boxing it is like being the fastest gun in the west. A lot of people are out to shoot you down, and even if you're faster on the draw than your opponent a stray bullet can cause a lot of damage. I went into the ring against Funches knowing that if I gave him half a chance he had a shot that could put me in trouble.

Terry's pre-fight instructions were that I should pace myself. 'Move around and jab with him,' he said. 'Hold back on your big punches unless you feel it's vital to let them go. I'd like to see you get some rounds under your belt. So only open up if you feel you have to.'

At 15 stone 7 pounds I had a stone weight advantage, and right from the first bell I felt fully in command - not only of the fight but of myself. In my early contests I was so tense and uptight that I would have struggled to tell you afterwards what punches I had thrown. But by this stage of my career I was really picking my punches and knew exactly what I was doing. I had always wondered how great golfers like Jack Nicklaus and Seve Ballesteros could recall every single shot they made in a round during major championships, but I was now discovering that I could almost pick my punches like a Nicklaus or a Ballesteros would pick their clubs. Mind you, I didn't have a caddy to hand them to me. I carry everything myself and it's just the unloading that I have to worry about.

It was the jab that I selected as the 'club' with which to tame Funches. For four rounds I hardly had it out of his face. At one stage he fell back into the ropes, and as he tried to start a counterattack got his right glove entangled in the top strand. I stood back while he freed himself and Funches signalled his thanks that I had not taken advantage. The fight game is a hard, hard business but there should always be room for sportsmanship.

At the end of the fourth round Terry let me off the leash. 'You can start throwing your combinations in this round,' he said.

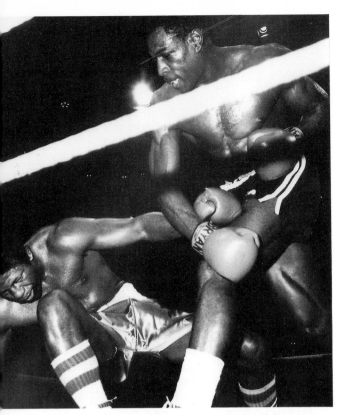

Barry Funches, the punching postman from New York, has just taken a first-class delivery on the jaw. I never allowed him to stamp his authority on the fight

'He's looked anxious the couple of times you have let your right go. So now let him feel the full weight of it. But remember to keep your left high because he's got a sneaky right that he's looking to land.'

It was unknown territory for me because it was the first time that I had gone past the fourth round, but I didn't feel in the slightest bit tired. I opened the fifth with another volley of left jabs just to make Funches think that it was going to be the same pattern as before. Then I suddenly stepped in sharply and threw a right uppercut that jolted his head back. His legs splayed and as he started falling to the canvas I followed on with a right hook.

Funches just beat the count, but was stumbling like a man on elasticated legs. I landed two more rights that sent him reeling sideways before referee Harry Gibbs waved me away and led Funches back to his corner.

I visited Funches in his dressing-room after the contest and found him to be a pleasant man. He said, surprisingly, that he had enjoyed the fight and he was kind enough to tell me: 'You're something special, man.'

He then gave me a list of fighters he reckoned I should meet as what he called stepping stones to the world title. It was thoughtful of him, but I reckoned I should leave that sort of thing to Terry. He knew exactly what he was doing. In fact he was managing magnificently, know what I mean?

FIGHT No. 17
Opponent: **Mike Jameson (USA)**
Venue: **De Vinci Manor, Chicago**
Date: **15 July, 1983**

As part of my educational trip to the United States in the summer of '83 I was matched with Mike Jameson, a former nightclub bouncer from California. My American debut took place in the unusual setting of the Chicago De Vinci Manor, a plush dance hall that was decorated with chandeliers and marble statues.

The fight was staged in the afternoon so that it could be screened 'live' in Britain by BBCtv, who loyally covered every one of my fights on my way to challenging for the world championship.

Chicago is known as the Windy City, but the fight went on in the middle of a heatwave. It was like a furnace in the ring under the scorching combination of the television and ring lights. Jameson had been a late starter as a professional boxer, switching from American football at the age of twenty-five. He had got his career off to an impressive start with a string of victories and his first-round victory over Ron Gibbs, one of my former opponents, was evidence that he could bang a bit.

Jameson then hit a losing run, and he made no secret of the fact that he saw a victory over me as a quick way of getting himself back into the reckoning as a potential contender. Like a lot of United States heavyweights he was curious to know more about me after I had been named 'Prospect of the Year' by *Ring Magazine*, which is the 'bible' of American boxing.

I was in terrific shape for the fight after working out for ten days at the Grossinger's Camp in New York State where I had sparred with highly rated heavyweights James 'Quick' Tillis, Jeff Sims and Mike Tyson. We were showing off the 'Best of British' to the Americans. British champions Barry McGuigan and my

stablemate at the time, Lloyd Honeyghan, were also on the bill. Barry impressed everybody with his power and finesse when he knocked out his first American opponent, Lavon McGowan, in the first round. Honeyghan survived a first-round knockdown to fight back and stop Kevin Austin, of Milwaukee, in the tenth and final round of a really hectic welterweight scrap. Both Barry and Lloyd served notice of their great potential, and both have since gone on to make their mark at world level, particularly featherweight champion McGuigan who is pound-for-pound one of the greatest fighters on either side of the Atlantic. He has been a marvellous advertisement for our sport and it was a privilege to have him as a companion in Chicago.

Jameson came into the ring for our fight with a thick growth of beard, which used to

Barry McGuigan will never get carried away with his incredible success. He impressed the American fight fans in Chicago with a devastating first-round knockout victory

be illegal. 'Just aim for the whiskers,' said Terry as I prepared to step out into the middle of the ring for my American debut.

I started cautiously behind a straight left and Jameson retreated, hiding his face behind a high guard. The Californian kept peeping at me between his gloves and seemed to be looking for an opening to launch a counterattack. Every time he shaped to throw a punch I just filled his face with my left glove, drilling in solid jabs and hooks.

Jameson had a complete change of tactics in the second round, charging at me with both fists swinging. I stepped inside and he banged away to my body, but I managed to block most of the blows on my elbows. Then, very deliberately, I threw what was my best combination of punches to date. I saw him lower his right and I unleashed a left hook to the point of his jaw, delivering it with a full turn of my hips. The effect on Jameson was startling. His right leg came up off the canvas as if he had trodden on broken glass.

He was falling sideways towards the canvas when I almost straightened him up with a right uppercut that was stage two of my combination. The punch came up from round about my knees, and as it landed under his chin he crashed backwards, out to the world.

Jameson was a real charmer of a character and we had a long chat after the fight. 'I honestly didn't see what hit me,' he told me. 'All I can tell you, Frank, is that you've got the kick of a mule in your fists. If you hit 'em, man, they've gotta go.'

Angelo Dundee, the trainer who had worked with both Muhammad Ali and Sugar Ray Leonard, was at the ringside and told reporters: 'This is the best heavyweight prospect from Britain in a long, long time.

They were calling me the Chicago hit man after this knockout of Mike Jameson. "If you hit 'em, they've gotta go," he told me after being counted out in the second round

123

He's got the sort of natural punching power that will cause problems for any heavyweight in the world. But having said that, I must point out that he has also got faults. He walks in, instead of gliding in on the balls of his feet, and he could get knocked cold with a left hook as he comes in. Bruno has tons of potential but he must be brought along slowly and not rushed.'

I noted what Mr Dundee had to say because I respect all that he has achieved as a trainer, but I still feel strongly that I can get more power into my punches if I have my leading foot firmly on the canvas rather than with the heel off the ground. Terry didn't need anybody to tell him that I shouldn't be rushed.

'As far as I'm concerned,' he told the press in Chicago, 'Frank is still wearing "'L" plates. 'There is a lot of pressure being put on me to match him with fighters out of the top ten, but I am not taking any notice.

'I agree it's necessary to move up in quality, but not so that he is suddenly out of his depth against far more experienced fighters. In this game, you don't go back to square one after a defeat. It can be disasterous, so you have to learn how to bring fighters along at the right pace. People can say and think what they like. I am not going to match Frank over his head.'

Asked what he thought of my performance against Jameson, Terry said: 'What thrilled me most about it was his professionalism. He was like a block of ice when he drilled in that right uppercut to finish his man. His temperament is now as impressive as his physique. It's hard to believe that this is a British heavyweight we're talking about, isn't it? I think he can go all the way. No, I *know* he can. But it will be done in our own good time.'

Terry caught me reading these quotes on the sports pages and leant over and whispered with that rascal's smile of his: 'Don't believe all you read in the newspapers.'

FIGHT No. 18
Opponent: Bill Sharkey (USA)
Venue: Wembley Arena
Date: 27 September, 1983

I was in training for my fight against Bill Sharkey when news came through that Scott LeDoux, my fifteenth opponent, had announced his retirement at the age of thirty-four and at the end of an eventful career during which he fought five world champions - George Foreman, Ken Norton, Mike Weaver, Leon Spinks and Larry Holmes.

Schoolteacher LeDoux said it was his defeat by me in his final fight that convinced him the time had come to hang up his gloves. Asked to list the hardest punchers he had met, LeDoux was kind enough to say that I rated among the top five punchers in the world. I was flattered but at the same time recalled a quote I had read by Earnie Shavers, who so nearly became world heavyweight champion when he knocked Larry Holmes down but not quite out in a storming title fight in 1979.

Shavers would come top of most lists if you were to have a poll as to who has been the hardest-hitting heavyweight of the last twenty years. He carried knockout drops in his right hand but once said: 'In a way getting so many of my early fights over so quickly worked against me. It meant that when I got in against better-class opponents I didn't know how to pace myself properly and I was running out of gas after six or seven rounds.'

This quote stuck in my memory, and I wondered how I would cope with a fight that went the distance. I thought that in Bill Sharkey we had found somebody who could possibly last the course. He had gone the distance with a noted puncher in Mike Weaver, and had held Scott LeDoux to a draw over ten rounds. So he obviously had stamina and also a reasonable fight record, winning twenty-three of his thirty professional contests.

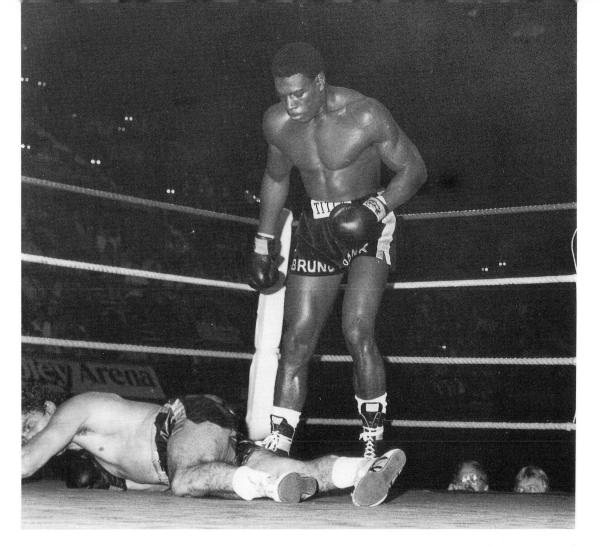

Bill Sharkey is flat out at my feet and my chances of getting some rounds under my belt have gone down with him

But on the night Bill Sharkey just wasn't big enough for the job. I was surprised to find him so small. At 13 stone 11 pounds he was having to concede nearly two stone to me and I had a considerable advantage in height and reach. I knew I needed experience against opponents of all shapes and sizes, but he didn't look much bigger than a light-heavyweight.

He came charging towards me at the first bell as if he really meant business. His head was down and he was swinging punches from all angles. I stood my ground in the centre of the ring and kept spearing down at him with my left.

The way he was ducking his head made him an inviting target for an uppercut. I picked my moment to let it go and brought the punch up from my knees as he rushed blindly in. The knuckle part of my glove connected with the point of his chin, and he collapsed face first to the canvas, leaving referee Roland Dakin with the job of counting to ten.

I went to see the New Yorker in his dressing-room after the fight and he wished me good luck and said: 'Scott LeDoux is right. You really are one of the world's hardest punchers.'

It was nice to hear but I still didn't know how I would cope if any of my fights went the distance.

FIGHT No. 19
Opponent: **Floyd Cummings (USA)**
Venue: **Royal Albert Hall**
Date: **11 October, 1983**

If you've ever been kicked by an elephant you might have a rough idea how I felt at the end of the first round of my fight against Floyd Cummings. I say an elephant because Cummings was nicknamed 'Jumbo', having the build of a bull elephant.

But before I tell you about the fight let me tell you about the man, who was nearly as incredible a character as Jeff Sims, the boxer I introduced in Chapter Eight.

At the age of seventeen, Cummings had been sentenced to a fifty-to-seventy-five-year jail sentence after being found guilty along with three others of the shooting of a grocer during a robbery in January 1967, when one Franklyn Bruno was six years old and running pretty wild in the backstreets of Wandsworth.

Being locked up was nothing new for Cummings. He was arrested for the first

This is the sort of overarm right with which 'Jumbo' Cummings gave me so much trouble. He was slipping inside my jab and countering over the top

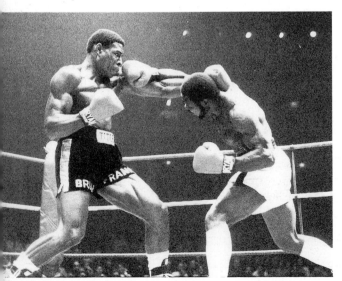

time when he was eight. His grandmother, who was bringing him up, told the police she couldn't handle him and he was sent to what he described as a kids' prison in Mississippi. I guess it was something like Oak Hall only on a larger scale.

It was in Stateville maximum security prison that Cummings first got hooked on boxing. He started off concentrating on weightlifting - which explains his stunning physique - and then switched to boxing after being discouraged to find that the top weights he could pump were way below the world records being set by Russian lifters.

A top amateur boxer called Billy 'Boy' Thompson arrived at the prison and Cummings was talked into taking him on. Thompson was 1970 Golden Gloves heavyweight champion and had beaten Ron Lyle and floored George Foreman. Cummings beat Thompson twice in behind-prison-walls amateur contests and it was then he decided that boxing was going to be his sport.

Cummings was released on parole after serving twelve years of his sentence and, aged twenty-nine, he immediately turned professional. He won his first fourteen fights before being outpointed by an outstanding prospect called Renaldo Snipes, who complained after the fight that Cummings had bitten him on the shoulder.

In his seventeenth contest he held former world champion Smokin' Joe Frazier to a draw. He then suffered four successive defeats against Larry Frazier, Mitchell Green, Tim Witherspoon and that other

It's the interval at the end of the first round and Terry Lawless and Frank Black are inquiring after my health after Jumbo's right had exploded on my jaw. I must admit that I had felt better

extraordinary character I was telling you about, Jeff Sims.

It was then that he was matched with me and everybody was agreed it would be easily my toughest test to date. But nobody guessed quite how tough it would be.

I weighed in at 15 stone 7 pounds and had a two-and-a-half-pounds weight advantage. Not that you would have guessed it looking at the muscular chest and shoulders of the 6 foot 2 inch tall Cummings who seemed as wide as a bus. He was surly and growling insults at the weigh-in, and didn't strike me as being exactly the nicest person in the world. Mind you, I hardly expected him to be Mr Goody-Two-Shoes!

The fight was televised live by BBC and I can give a clear account of the first round because I have watched the replay dozens of times. I kept Cummings on the end of my jab for most of the round. He was concentrating on trying to slip inside my lead and throw clubbing punches to my head. But I could see them coming and was able to block them or step out of range.

The round was into its last minute when Cummings drove me to the ropes. I threw a left hook counter which he managed to duck beneath. He had his head down and I - amateurishly, I have to admit - was standing too stiff and erect, with my head held high and my chin sticking out as if to dry. While almost crouching in front of me Cummings suddenly threw an over-the-top right that caught me flush on the jaw. I can only describe this clearly because of the television replays. To be honest, at the time I didn't know what had hit me. He almost bowled the punch as if he was Michael Holding letting fly with a bouncer. I was out on my feet but, thank God, the bell rang before he could throw a follow-up punch that would almost certainly have knocked me over for the first time in my career.

As referee Mike Jacobs caught hold of me Terry appeared at my side as if he had come up through a trapdoor in the ring. I think he must have set some sort of world record for getting through the ropes and into the ring. He steered me back to the corner

where he, along with Jimmy Tibbs and Frank Black, worked overtime to bring me round. My senses were coming back and when Terry asked me how many fingers he was holding up I was able to tell him 'two'. As I prepared to go out for the second round my head was still spinning but I was able to digest Terry's clear instructions: 'Keep that jab pumping out and your chin tucked in to your shoulder. Don't let him get on top of you. And don't get caught on the ropes.'

The second round was one of the toughest I have ever known, and I had to reach down deep into my heart to make myself get through it. 'You're not going to let this man beat you,' I kept saying to myself as I bit hard on my gumshield and tried to avoid the big bombs that were coming my way.

Cummings was throwing everything at me. I tried to keep him off with my jab, but my timing and rhythm was out of sync. I just couldn't get it together and he hit me with at least six good, clean shots during that nightmare three minutes.

When I returned to the corner, Jimmy Tibbs greeted me with the words: 'You're going to win this Frank. The feller's punched himself out.'

He could have fooled me, but Terry added: 'It's true, Frank. He's hit you with his best shots and it's broken his heart that you're still standing. He's puffing and panting like an old man. Now you can begin to take charge. Shorten your punches and you'll find him easy to hit.'

I did as I was told and started to throw short jabs and hooks that thudded through the defence of Cummings, who suddenly found there was not a long left that he could slip inside. My confidence came back as I realised a lot of the sting had gone out of his punches, and by the fourth round it was Cummings who was beginning to rock on his heels as I unloaded some of my heaviest ammunition.

He was getting so desperate by the fifth round that he started introducing rough-house tactics, holding my arms in a vice-like grip every time he got to close quarters.

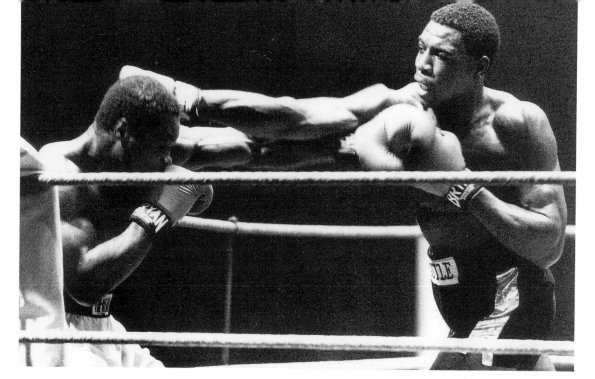

My comeback has begun and this time it is Jumbo who is in trouble as I start finding the range with my big bombs

Twice he tried deliberately to butt me, and referee Mike Jacobs gave him a stern warning. I could feel the strength draining out of him in the sixth round - the farthest I had been taken as a professional - and every time we went into a clinch he was breathing so heavily that he sounded like an old steam engine.

Terry sent me out for the seventh with orders to 'go for it'. All his experience as a cornerman told him that Cummings was ready to be taken. Twice I measured him with my left before throwing follow-through rights that made him stagger. He left himself wide open, and I put everything into a right hook that caught him on the side of the jaw and sent him sprawling to the canvas.

He pulled himself up at seven but then immediately went down again on one knee and the referee signalled that it was all over. I had passed my toughest test.

It was suggested in some quarters that the way I reacted when Cummings landed his right hand punch in the first round proved I couldn't take a punch. What rubbish! I know - because I was the man on the receiving end - that nine out of ten heavyweights would have been flattened by that punch. It was a real cracker and the fact that I was able to recover from it and go on and win satisfied those in the know that I could take a punch.

I thanked referee Mike Jacobs after the fight for the way he held on to me at the end of the first round. He told me that there was so much noise from the crowd that he only just managed to hear the bell. I wonder how differently this story would have read had he not heard it? I don't think I want to spend too much time considering that point.

I can't let this report of my nineteenth fight pass without praise for the way Terry, Jimmy Tibbs and Frank Black worked in the corner. They are the best corner team in the business, and their professionalism and expert advice makes all the difference when the going gets tough.

The big lesson I had learned - and have never forgotten - is don't ever stick your chin out like I did in that first round. It's a dangerous thing to do. If you've ever been kicked by an elephant you'll know what I mean!

129

FIGHT No. 20
Opponent: Walter Santemore (USA)
Venue: Royal Albert Hall
Date: 6 December, 1983

The public reaction to my recovery against 'Jumbo' Cummings was astonishing. I received hundreds of letters from complete strangers congratulating me on the way I had fought back, and people kept coming up to me in the street for a week after the fight telling me what a great job I had done.

But I was far from happy with my performance, and I went back into the gym with trainer Jimmy Tibbs and worked overtime at ironing out the fault that so nearly led to disaster against Cummings.

Jimmy had me sparring in front of a full-length mirror and nagged me every time my chin came up as I threw jabs. 'Tuck the chin in,' he kept shouting until it became second nature for me to get my chin down behind my shoulder each time I threw the left lead.

There was no way I was going to give Walter Santemore a glimpse of my chin in my next fight. He was not a noted big puncher, but the fact that he had outpointed one of the modern greats in Earnie Shavers was a warning to me that he had to be taken very seriously indeed, despite some of the critics rubbishing him as 'just a sparring partner.'

Santemore had worked as number one sparring partner to world heavyweight championship challenger Gerry Cooney and that to me meant he was to be respected rather than ridiculed. Cooney would not have hired him unless he considered that he was durable and could stand up to his heavy hitting.

There were a lot of defeats on the long record of thirty-two-year-old Santemore but only by the very best heavyweights around. Top-class fighters of the calibre of John Tate, James 'Quick' Tillis, Jeff Sims and 'Bonecrusher' Smith. My showing against Cummings had underlined what Terry had been saying for months: that I still had a lot to learn. Santemore looked to be the ideal type of opponent to help me get vital experience. He was a former policeman from New Orleans who knew every trick in the book and some that have never been published.

At the weigh-in, Santemore - 6 feet 5 inches tall - weighed in at just over 16 stone three pounds, which gave him a weight advantage of nearly half a stone. 'Back home I'm known as "Mad Dog",' he told me after stepping off the scales. 'Tonight, man, you're gonna find out why.'

But I reckoned he was more of an old fox than a mad dog and I refused to fall for his clowning tricks in the first round. He was doing a sort of heavy-footed Ali shuffle that amused the crowd, but I wasn't in the ring for a laugh. For me, boxing is a serious business.

All the time he was pretending to clown he was looking for the chance to throw the sort of right hands that he had seen land from Jumbo Cummings when shown a video of our fight. I was well prepared for them and, with my chin tucked into my shoulder, stabbed him off with my left jab. One wild right whacked into my back, and another missed the target by at least a foot as I stepped out of range and then countered with a left-right to the head. As he returned to his corner at the end of this opening round Santemore had blood seeping from a cut under his left eye.

There was less dancing and more punching from Santemore in the second round. He tried to rough me up inside and caught me high on the head with a couple of sneaky rights, and then put everything into a right uppercut. I saw it coming and got

Walter Santemore had been trying to clown around with me by doing the Ali shuffle. But now he was doing a sort of break dance on the canvas

away fast, and Santemore spun off balance as the punch missed its intended target. I was now on red alert and tossed my first big right of the night. It landed too high to do any real damage but carried enough force to send Santemore back into a neutral corner. I tried to follow up, but he showed what a cunning old so-and-so he was by tying me up and rolling and smothering as I tried to pin him on the ropes.

My punches were beginning to have an effect, and referee Roland Dakin was starting to look anxiously at a cut above as well as below the American's left eye.

Santemore knew his time was running out and came gunning for me in the third round. He forced me on the retreat with a volley of swinging lefts and rights which were falling short. After this attempt to finish me off had failed he went back to his clowning tactics, winding his right up like a baseball pitcher and then throwing the left.

All the time this was going on I was waiting patiently for the chance to get in with a really telling right. The opening came in the last seconds of the round, and I clipped him on the jaw with a short, chopping right hook. He went over on his side but was up almost straight away as the bell rang.

Showman Santemore tried to kid me into thinking I was not worrying him by starting the fourth round with a sort of clumsy tap dance. But I quickly had him doing a break dance on the canvas. I measured him with a left lead, and then put all my bodyweight behind a follow-through right that landed high on the side of Santemore's left cheek. He crashed on his back and I knew that my night's was work finished. With a great show of courage, Santemore managed to get himself into a standing position at a count of nine, but he was in no position to defend himself and Mr Dakin signalled that he had been knocked out.

It was my last fight of 1983 and Terry told the press: 'Frank has had a marvellous year, but 1984 is going to be even better.'

We didn't know then that the 'Bonecrusher' was waiting around the corner.

FIGHT No. 21
Opponent: **Juan Figueroa (Argentina)**
Venue: **Wembley Arena**
Date: **13 March, 1984**

Juan Figueroa was lined up as my first opponent of 1984. The reporters punching their typewriter keys dismissed him as a push-over, but it was me who had to do the real punching and I treated him with full respect.

He was the heavyweight champion of Argentina, stood six and a half feet tall and weighed in at just three and a half pounds under fifteen stone. I wonder if those writers who had described him as a push-over would have fancied doing the pushing?

Figueroa worked in his family's market gardening business and was nicknamed the 'Giant of the Market'. He had been a professional since 1976 and while his record was dotted with several defeats I also noticed when looking through it that he had stopped fourteen opponents on his way to twenty victories.

The 30-year-old Argentinian had been recently fighting out of Atlantic City, which meant he would have been getting the best possible sparring practice in what has become a busy American fight centre. So taking all these things into account I was determined not to make the mistake of under-rating Figueroa.

All those people who had counted out Figueroa before a punch had been thrown

Facing page: Top referee Harry Gibbs counted "nine...ten..out" in two successive fights involving me. That's Harry at the top tolling off the ten seconds after I had flattened Juan Figueroa in the first round. And that's Harry signalling the first (and only, please God) knockout defeat of my career against 'Bonecrusher' Smith. You win some, you lose some...know what I mean, 'Arry?

were no doubt claiming they had been proved right when I won the fight in just sixty-seven seconds. But in fairness to the 'Giant of the Market' I should stress that it was two good whacks to the jaw that put him over and out.

I measured him with a left jab, then let go with the combination that Jimmy Tibbs had helped me polish in the gymnasium - the left hook and right cross. Figueroa folded in front of me, and I knew from the moment of my double connection that he had lost all interest in the fight. Referee Harry Gibbs went through the formality of counting him out while I stood in a neutral corner willing him to get up. It was frustrating for me because I was looking forward to a much longer fight. I wanted to try out all the new punch patterns that I had been learning in the three months since my last fight.

A lot of criticism came our way over that fight, but Terry told me: 'Shut your ears to them, Frank. They just don't realise the power that you are carrying in your fists.'

But my pride was demanding that I should be given a real test by somebody who was well established on the heavyweight scene. Terry agreed that my apprenticeship was over and 'live' American television was arranged for my next fight to give me vital projection in the United States. Out of the opposite corner would be coming a fighter called James 'Bonecrusher' Smith. Now there was a name to conjure with....

FIGHT No. 22
Opponent: **James 'Bonecrusher' Smith (USA)**
Venue: **Wembley Arena**
Date: **13 May, 1984**

It was while he was serving in the U.S. Army in Germany that James Smith became known as 'Bonecrusher.' On a disasterous night at Wembley (Sunday, Bloody Sunday - the unlucky thirteenth) it proved a sickeningly appropriate nickname. And they were my bones that were crushed. 'Bonecrusher' became 'Brunocrusher' and pitched my career into a crisis.

Smith had never laced on a boxing glove in his life until he was twenty-three. He had concentrated on basketball while at high school and college in his hometown of Magnolia, North Carolina. Sergeant Smith started boxing for his Army base and picked up his nickname after reeling off twenty-five knockout victories in thirty-five amateur contests.

After leaving the Army, Smith became a guard at Raleigh maximum security jail and started boxing professionally to help feed his young family. He was not 100 per cent fit for his debut and was stopped in four rounds after coming in as a late substitute against hot prospect James Broad.

Smith was encouraged by his performance because he had given Broad a lot of trouble until - as he put it - 'I ran out of steam because I had not trained properly.' He wondered what he could achieve if he got himself into good shape. The answer was thirteen successive victories, and the last nine inside the distance. His fifteenth professional fight was to be back in Europe where he had first started boxing. And waiting to face him in a ten-round international contest was one Frank Bruno.

The right from 'Bonecrusher' that finally crushed me after I had stupidly got myself trapped on the ropes in the nightmare tenth round

The night started disasterously for our EastEnders stable. Mark Kaylor, British middleweight champion and in my opinion one of the most talented fighters in the world, was knocked down five times before being stopped in the seventh round by Philadelphia power-puncher Buster Drayton. This shock defeat dropped a heavy cloud of gloom on our dressing-room. It made me even more determined to beat 'Bonecrusher' and put a smile back on Terry's face.

NBC of America were showing the fight live on their coast-to-coast sports programme and I knew a good performance against 29-year-old Smith would increase my earning potential by at least another 'nought'. He was equally keen to do well because even though he was short on professional experience his name was already being mentioned as a world title contender.

Smith was an inch taller than me, well-muscled and, at 16 stone 3 pounds, outweighing me by five and a half pounds. I won't bore you with a long breakdown of the fight. To be honest, it was never a classic. Perhaps there was too much at stake for both of us. I never really got into any rhythm but managed to dictate most of the rounds with a left jab that was rarely out of Smith's face. He fought crudely at times, but was always threatening danger with looping rights that travelled in a similar arc to the punch with which 'Jumbo' Cummings caused me problems.

We had both used up a lot of energy by the time the fight was into the eighth round, which was unknown territory for me. Smith's right eye was swollen and he was looking the worse for wear, but for the first time in my professional career I was feeling tired to the point of exhaustion. Terry, Jimmy Tibbs and Frank Black were having to give me pep talks in the corner because they knew I was beginning to feel sorry for myself.

It wasn't Smith's punches that had got to me. He had hardly hurt me at all. It was the tension. The occasion. It had drained me of my usual strength. These are not excuses I'm making. I just want you to realise how a fighter feels when he's up there in the ring and so much is at stake.

In the interval before the last round Terry told me: 'Don't get involved. He knows he has got to knock you out to win. Just keep that jab pumping into his face. You've got the fight won. Don't do anything silly. Box.'

Bruno, stupid Bruno, didn't listen. Even though I was winning the fight by a mile, I knew I hadn't impressed anybody - the Wembley fans or the American television viewers - and I decided I would give them something to remember me by. Well, I certainly did that, but not in the way I intended.

I went out for that final round with one thought in mind - to knock 'Bonecrusher's' block off. But he had his own script in mind. As I went hunting him with a big right he swung a left hook to the side of my jaw that knocked me back onto the ropes. Suddenly I felt as if I had fallen down a deep, black hole. If I had been more experienced I would - and should - have gone down for a count while my head cleared. But a mixture of inexperience and stupid pride made me try to stay upright as Smith pounded me with fourteen punches. I promise you I didn't count them at the time. I've watched action replays of the fight so many times that every blow is cemented into my memory. When I watch the video of the fight it is like looking at somebody else trapped on those ropes. I force myself to keep watching it so that I'll know what to do if ever I should be in that position again. One thing's for sure, I won't hang around on the ropes. That was a novice-like thing to do.

Again, my critics jumped in with the view that 'Bonecrusher' had proved in that final round that I had a weak chin. I disagree (but then I would, wouldn't I!). If my chin had been weak that first left hook would have knocked me down and out. The

'Bonecrusher' tells how it was at the post-fight Press conference. From the look on my face you can see that I am obviously still finding it hard to believe that I lost

fourteen punches that followed from one of the biggest punchers in the heavyweight division would have knocked over a horse.

Finally I fell sideways to the canvas. I had watched Harry Gibbs count out several of my opponents, including Juan Figueroa in my last contest. Now he was a blurred figure counting over me. I could hear his voice shouting out the count but it seemed to be coming from the end of a tunnel. All my instincts were trying to tell me to drag myself up. My heart was willing, but my limbs no longer seemed to belong to me. I've seen on the video how I tried to pull myself back up by holding on to the ropes, but I had lost all sense of direction. By the

time I had focused sufficiently to realise exactly where I was and what was happening it was too late, and Harry Gibbs was shouting above the roar of the crowd: '...eight...nine...out!'

That final volley of punches from Smith had opened a gash inside my mouth which needed eight stitches. But the physical pain was nothing to the mental blows I had taken. What I didn't realise at the time was how my defeat - coming immediately after Mark Kaylor's disaster - had knocked Terry for six.

He looked shell-shocked, and his immediate reaction was that he was going to quit the fight game. 'It's taking too much out of me,' he said to me quietly in the early hours of Monday morning as we sadly discussed the nightmare we had been through. 'I just can't take any more.'

It was only then that I realised how Terry

137

had felt every blow as if he himself was in the ring. He looks on his fighters like second sons and he suffers agonies with us all. Suddenly, all the pressure had got on top of him.

We were due at a post-fight press conference the next morning. At first Terry said he wasn't going to go. It was then that I found a sudden faith in myself. I like to think it came from God, but I am not going to push the point because I don't want people to think I am some sort of religious crank.

I spent an hour doing the sort of motivating for Terry that he has done for me throughout my career. 'If you quit, I'll quit,' I said. 'But neither of us are going to quit because we've come too far to give it all up now. We'll look back on this defeat one day as a blessing in disguise. You've been saying all along that I am not ready for the top boys. Now you have been proved right. You can bring me along at your pace. If I had beaten Smith I would have been pitched in with Mike Weaver next, and we both know I'm not yet ready for that kind of fight. What I do know, Tel, is that one day I am going to become heavyweight champion of the world. And I want you in the corner with me because I can't do it without you. So come on, let's get to that press conference and tell the world that this isn't the end for Bruno but a new beginning.'

Yes, I really was that articulate. I found all the right words at the right time and convinced Terry that he had to keep going. This is what he said at the press conference when we turned up an hour and a half late: 'I have to be honest with you and admit that if it wasn't for the big feller I wouldn't be here today. He bullied me into coming. He has said that if he can carry on after the heartbreak of last night, then I can as well. 'If you quit, then I'll quit,' he said to me. And I think he really meant it. I have been through the worst night of my life. It was a nightmare and I didn't think I had the will to carry on. I get emotionally involved with my boys. I know I shouldn't but I can't do the job any other way. Thanks to Frank and his enormous faith in both himself and in me the show goes on, folks. But it will be at my pace. He remains the best heavyweight prospect this country has ever had and he will be back.'

The one good thing about it all was that Bonecrusher's success could not have happened to a nicer feller. I found him a real charmer and I was delighted for him when he got a crack at the world championship then held by Larry Holmes. Six months after his victory over me he gave Holmes all the trouble he could handle before being stopped in twelve rounds.

My time would come. Bonecrusher had just temporarily held back the hands of the clock.

And that was doing Terry and me a favour, know what I mean?

FIGHT No. 23
Opponent: **Ken Lakusta (Canada)**
Venue: **Wembley Arena**
Date: **25 September, 1984**

Even my severest critics had to admit I had chosen a tough road back when they heard I was matched with Canadian iron-man Ken Lakusta in a ten-round eliminator for the Commonwealth heavyweight title.

It's difficult to explain, but I was a different person from the one knocked out in the same Wembley ring a little over four months earlier. I was more mature and my confidence, rather than shrinking, had grown. Terry was more aware of this than anybody and it explains why he agreed to a match that many people thought could have been as tough as the 'Bonecrusher' fight.

I made the 'Bonecrusher' defeat work for me. It was all down to the positive

When you've gotta go, you've gotta go. This is the 'nuclear' right that ended Ken Lakusta's interest in our Commonwealth championship eliminator

thinking that Terry had been teaching me. I convinced myself that getting beaten was the best thing that could have happened to me. Now I didn't have to get uptight about protecting my unbeaten record, and I could go into the ring without the pressure of having to impress people. In future, I decided I would try only to impress myself, Terry, my trainers Jimmy Tibbs and Frank Black, and - oh, yes - my opponent.

I was much happier in myself and more relaxed. Somehow, 'Bonecrusher' had managed to knock the tension and tightness out of me. Defeat, I thought, would be like the end of the world. I didn't think I would be able to look myself in the mirror or into the faces of friends, relatives and fans. I got a bit of stick from youngsters, who would shout insulting remarks when I was out on training runs ('Watch out, Bruno, the

Thank God, I'm back and winning. I went down on my knees to give thanks for my combeack victory over Ken Lakusta

couldn't wait to get back into the ring to show off the new Bruno.

Lakusta was noted for his strength and aggressive style of fighting. Just a year earlier he had given talented Commonwealth champion Trevor Berbick a hell of a battle before going down to a tenth round defeat. But I was in no mood to give him a look-in.

For the first time in my career I weighed in at more than sixteen stone - one and a half pounds over to be exact, which gave me a full stone advantage over the rugged Canadian. At twenty-two I was still a growing boy, and I knew that at just over sixteen stone I would be able to produce my full punching power.

Lakusta quickly discovered that for himself. He came rushing at me in the opening seconds like a wild bull, but I pulled him up in his tracks with a series of short hooks and uppercuts. Following my 'Bonecrusher' defeat he obviously thought he was going to catch me low on confidence and resistance, but when he landed with a long, swinging right he was shocked to find me responding with a left hook-right cross combination that forced him to hold on to me for dear life.

There was a hint of desperation in Lakusta's work at the start of the second round. He was crowding me and throwing wild punches that suggested he wanted to get things over and done with as quickly as possible. I gave him his wish. After stabbing him off with jarring straight lefts I picked my spot for what I have nicknamed my 'nuclear' right - a long hook-cum-cross that crashed on to the side of his jaw. He dropped in a neutral corner where referee John Coyle counted him out at the halfway point of the second round.

I instinctively dropped to my knees in a gesture of thanks to God, and the standing ovation I got from the spectators convinced me that the 'Bonecrusher' defeat had done me no harm whatsoever. Bruno - the new Bruno - was back in business.

Bonecrusher's after you!'), but mostly I found people sympathetic and supportive. In fact I was amazed by the public reaction. The postman brought hundreds of letters to my home, the gym and to Terry's home from people we had never met, but offering words of encouragement and support. A lot of the the letters were from boxing fans, but many came from caring people who identified with my desire and determination to make something of myself. Some of the letters were signed by entire members of a family. I wanted to reach out and cuddle every one of them for showing that they still believed in me.

It all helped me get into a better frame of mind, and Laura will tell you that I was suddenly an easier person to live with. The lifting of the tension meant I was able to function better in the gymnasium, and I

FIGHT No. 24
Opponent: **Jeff Jordan**
Venue: **Royal Albert Hall**
Date: **6, November, 1984**

My fight with Jeff Jordan was one of the weirdest contests in which I have ever been involved. He was, to put it mildly, an odd character.

We expected a tough test from him because his record before fighting me was quite respectable. He had won seventeen of twenty fights since turning professional six months before me, and as eleven of his victories had been inside the distance there was plenty of evidence to suggest he could whack a bit.

There's no hiding place in the ring. Jeff Jordan tries to shelter behind his gloves but I find a way through with a meaty left

He had not been fighting household names exactly, but that was a comment that had been made about me enough times for me to appreciate that he had been learning the trade. 'I've come to win,' he said at the weigh-in where he scaled a few ounces inside fourteen and a half stone. I scaled a heaviest-ever 16 stone 2 pounds and towered over him.

Jordan, who was nicknamed Joltin' Jeff, looked up at me and said: 'You don't frighten me, sucker.'

He was from Columbus, Ohio, the hometown of the 'Golden Bear' of golf, Jack Nicklaus. The way he was talking before the fight I wondered if I was about to

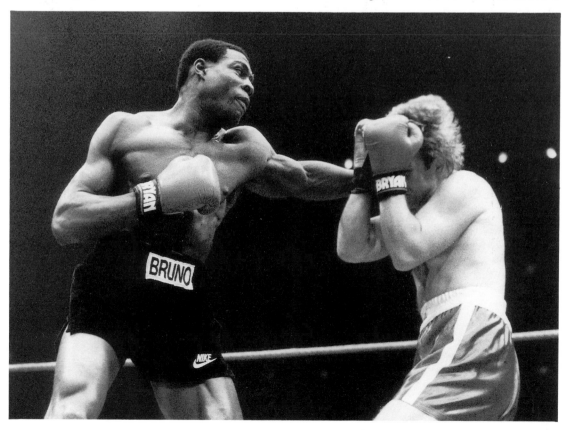

meet the 'Grizzly Bear'.

My fight plan was to keep him on the end of my left jab until I had seen what he had to offer. For the first minute I hardly had my left glove out of his face. He was threatening all sorts of things with swinging counter punches that were falling well short. As I drove him back towards his corner, one of his seconds shouted: 'Come on, Jeff baby, let's get acquainted.'

Jeff 'Baby's' face was beginning to redden from the efforts of my left glove, but he didn't seem in the slightest bit concerned. 'You ain't got nothin', sucker,' he told me as we went into a clinch.

I don't believe in talking in the ring. I like to save my breath for fighting. My reply was to unload four heavy rights that all landed on target and brought up a nasty swelling under Jordan's left eye. He shook his head at me at the bell, as much as to say 'you haven't hurt me.' But I wasn't the slightest bit taken in by his act. I also knew that I had not really opened up yet, so Jeff 'Baby' had some surprises coming his way.

Goodness knows what was going on in Jordan's corner, but I don't think they had quite the same professionalism that Terry, Jimmy Tibbs and Frank Black show in every fight. I was told afterwards that the final instruction from his corner as he came out for round two was: 'If he tags you, run like hell.'

I caught him with an uppercut that made him buckle at the knees. But he didn't run like hell. Instead he grabbed me in a sort of grizzly bear hold. 'Is that the best you can do, sucker?' he said. He stumbled as I wrestled away from his clutches, but there was no count. I hit him with a series of lefts and rights, and a left hook off a jab forced him to hold on again. He was shifting a lot of punishment and seemed to be almost enjoying it.

Jordan just wasn't in the fight. He was hardly landing any blows, and he seemed intent only on survival. The crowd were booing and slow-handclapping the stocky American's lack of effort. Referee Sid Nathan went to his corner at the end of the round and politely asked him to make an effort to join in the fight. I was told later that Jordan replied: 'Hell, ref, I've come to win. That sucker ain't seen nuthin' yet.'

But Jordan had nothing to show me but blind courage. I rocked him with long-range lefts and rights, and he made a brave attempt to fight back but never once got in range with his desperate punches. A right hook opened a gash over his left eye, and as I poured punches in without reply Mr Nathan pushed us apart and said: 'I've seen enough, thank you.'

I got the impression Jordan was relieved to be rescued. As my arm was raised in victory he said: 'You couldn't knock me down, sucker.'

As far as Joltin' Jeff Jordan was concerned, that was some sort of a triumph.

FIGHT No. 25
Opponent: **Phil Brown (USA)**
Venue: **Wembley Arena**
Date: **27 November, 1984**

There's an old saying that 'it takes two to tango.' In boxing, it takes two men to make a fight. Phil Brown didn't come to Wembley to fight but only to survive, and he gave me just about the most frustrating night of my life.

I got a hell of a lot of stick from the critics over my performance in this fight. I hold up my hands and admit that a lot of the criticism was deserved. But I don't think the people knocking me took into account the fact that it is really difficult to perform well against an opponent who is thinking only of stopping you from getting into any sort of rhythm.

Brown smothered and covered, twisted and turned, ducked and dived and clutched and grabbed...he did just about everything but fight. He had learnt all the aggravating tricks of the trade in the penitentiary back home in New Orleans where boxing had saved him from following a downhill run to a life on the wrong side of the law.

He had a respectable ring record, winning twenty-two fights and drawing two in a long unbeaten run, and the fact that he had outpointed the once highly-rated Jimmy Young was proof that he was a capable fighter. His undefeated record had been wrecked in his last fight when he came up against former world title contender Gerry Cooney, who was making a comeback in the unlikely place of Anchorage, Alaska. According to reports that I read of their September 1984 fight Brown hardly threw a punch before being knocked down and out in the fourth round.

He seemed just as reluctant to throw punches against me. It seemed an odd way for him to fight because at 6 foot 3 inches and 15 stone 5 pounds he must have had a lot of power in his body. But all he was

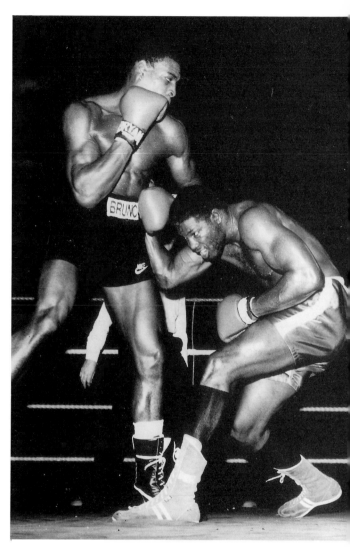

Phil Brown ducked and dived, smothered and covered and did everything but fight as he became the first opponent to take me the distance

concerned with from the first bell was taking avoiding action. He fought on the retreat and every time I tried to open up he would suddenly trap my gloves by holding,

143

or twist like an eel so that I became tangled up in his arms as I missed with attempted punches to the head.

Referee Larry O'Connell was as frustrated as the jeering fans, but none of them was as frustrated as me. In the fifth round the referee called 'time out' and told both Brown and me: 'The public deserve better than this. Let's see a fight. Come on now.'

Well I was doing my best to make it a fight, but Brown just wasn't interested and he continued with his negative tactics. For the first time in my career I was taken the full distance. There were no knockdowns and I had Brown in real trouble only a couple of times throughout the fight. His defensive, spoiling tactics had drawn all the sting from me.

The referee scored it 100 points to me and 95 to Brown, which meant I had won every round. But I was anything but satisfied with my performance, although Terry - positive as ever - pointed out that I had at least now experienced what it was like to be taken the distance, and I had done it without taking any punishment at all.

I knew in my heart that I had tried to make a fight of it. But Brown just didn't want to tango, know what I mean?

FIGHT No. 26
Opponent: Lucien Rodriguez (France)
Venue: Wembley Arena
Date: 27 March, 1985

Two years all but a day before this fight at Wembley Lucien Rodriguez had challenged Larry Holmes for the world heavyweight championship, and he had given an excellent account of himself before losing on points over twelve rounds. He had twice won the European title and had made six successful defences, including a convincing points victory over British champion David Pearce. In short, Monsieur Rodriguez looked to be my toughest opponent to date.

It was a vital contest for me because I was one fight away from challenging Anders Eklund for his European championship. The title fight had been signed up and this put extra pressure on me because I knew I daren't slip up against the vastly-experienced Rodriguez. The giant Swede was at the Wembley ringside on a spying mission, and I wanted to produce a performance that would cost him sleepless nights.

Rodriguez, born in Casablanca in 1951, was a vastly experienced campaigner who had turned professional back in 1973 when I was still at Oak Hall School day-dreaming about one day becoming world heavyweight champion. He was noted for his skilful boxing rather than his punching power, out-maneuvering opponents with intelligent tactics and clever ringcraft. In preparation for his fight with me he had taken a warm-up contest against a useful Yugoslav called Dragomir Popovic, and he had stopped him in eight rounds.

It was his twenty-first inside-the-distance victory, and in an eight-year career he had been beaten just nine times. I was to be his fiftieth opponent. I got good inside information on Rodriguez from Neville Meade, who was my 'EastEnders' stablemate when he won the British heavyweight championship. Neville had been the first man to beat Rodriguez in 1975 when he stopped him in the third round of a non-title fight in Paris. 'He's a slippery customer who likes to try to dictate the fight from the centre of the ring,' Neville told me. 'I got to him by shooting my right hand over his left lead.'

I noticed on video that David Pearce had also given him big problems with his right hand shots in their European title fight, and I worked extra hard in training on my left-right combination punches. I trained for speed as well as power because I thought I might have to do some chasing before I could catch up with the Frenchman. At the weigh-in I scaled a few ounces over 15 stone 12 pounds, the lightest I had been for several months. But I still had a weight advantage over Rodriguez of nearly a stone.

The fight started as I expected with Rodriguez 'getting on his bike' and circling backwards around the ring behind a light, flicking left. I was content to follow him for the opening two minutes, watching warily for any sneaky rights while I kept thudding a much harder left than his against his head. He made the mistake of backing away to the ropes and was unable to retreat any further as I let go with my first serious rights of the fight. I made him sag into the ropes with a right uppercut and followed with a solid right hook. It seemed to take several seconds for the power of the punches to take effect.

Suddenly he bowed forward and slowly sank to the canvas as I threw a right-left-right combination to the head. Referee Harry Gibbs signalled for me to go to a neutral corner as he took up the count. Rodriguez rose with great reluctance at the

I love Lucien! I always try to make friends with my opponents after our fights. Lucien Rodriguez is no doubt thinking here that he wished I had shown a little of this friendship during our brief encounter

count of nine, and as I stepped forward he shook his head and waved a fist in surrender, clearly indicating that he'd had enough, *'merci beaucoup'.*

I gave Rodriguez a consoling cuddle, and he told me in broken English: 'You next champion of Europe.' That made me wonder what Anders Eklund was thinking as he sat in his ringside seat.

Eklund came to see me in the dressing-room after the fight and we shook hands for the photographers. 'You beat an old man tonight,' he said. 'I am young and I have a strong chin, you'll see.'

'Just make sure you turn up, old chap,' I said in an exaggerated English accent. 'We can make a fortune together.'

Little did I realise then the heartache I was going to have to suffer before he did finally turn up for our European championship match.

FIGHT No. 27
Opponent: **Anders Eklund (Sweden)**
Venue: **Wembley Arena**
Date: **1 October, 1985**

There were times when it looked as if I would be more likely to meet Anders Eklund in the high court than the ring. First of all we were due to fight in April, 1985. This was called off when Eklund claimed he had damaged a hand. Promoters Mike Barrett and Mickey Duff won the purse bidding for the fight with an offer over £200,000. They rescheduled the fight for Wembley on June 25, but this was postponed following a dispute over television fees with Eklund's manager, Mogens Palle.

It was one of the most annoying and aggravating times of my life. All I wanted to do was get on with the fight and I kept bringing myself to a peak in training only to find further delays. I vowed to take my frustration and anger out on Eklund, but to be fair to him he was - like me - just a pawn in the politics of boxing (or, as a former British champion once said, 'we boxers are just prawns in the game').

The fight was finally arranged for Wembley in the autumn, which meant that by the time I climbed into the ring I would have gone eleven months with less than a round of action. I spent the time getting myself tuned to perfect fitness in the gymnasium, and I sparred dozens of rounds during which I sharpened my punch combinations and increased and improved the variety of them. My aim was to be less predictable, and I also worked hard at tightening my defence and learning how to tie opponents up at close quarters.

Thanks to the irritating postponements, I found it easy to motivate myself for the fight

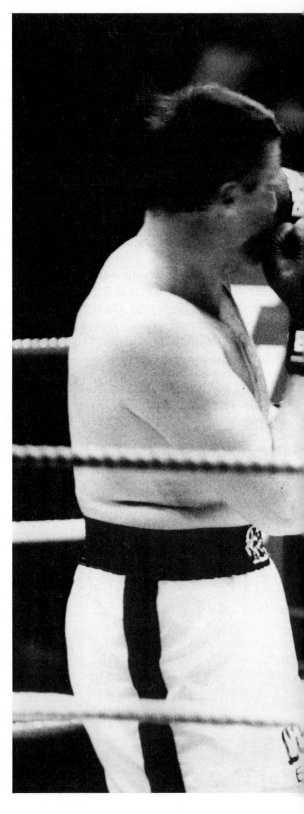

Right is might. This is the first of the rights that blasted the European championship away from Anders Eklund

146

by making Eklund the target for my anger. And the fact that he was walking off with the lion's share of the purse (more than £120,000) further helped put me in the mood to punish him. It was just as well I had a reason to be annoyed with twenty-seven-year-old Eklund because, to be honest, it would have been very easy to have really liked the man. He was a gentle giant outside the ring, quietly spoken and very polite and intelligent. All his fighting had to be done outside his homeland of Sweden where professional boxing is banned.

He was certainly the biggest opponent I have ever met. In fact I doubt if there have been many bigger champions in the history of boxing. He stood a fraction over 6 feet 6 inches tall and usually weighed in at just under seventeen stone. But he had seen what my power punching had done to Lucien Rodriguez, and decided that he would have a better chance of standing up to my punches if he increased his body bulk. He weighed in for our fight at a mammoth seventeen stone six-and-a-half pounds. I came in at just half a pound over sixteen stone.

I was able to get a good look at Eklund when he won the European championship with an impressive fourth round stoppage of the previously unbeaten Norwegian Steffen Tangstad. Their title fight was staged in Copenhagen in March, 1985, and I was invited to watch it 'live' in the ITV sports studio in London.

Eklund destroyed Tangstad with some dynamite punches that showed he had completely recovered from a startling first round defeat by Liverpudlian Noel Quarless and a points set-back against old Joe Bugner. I made careful note that Eklund strongly favoured his right which he threw in a similar straight-over-the-top style to Ingemar Johansson, the last Swedish heavyweight to dominate Europe (and for a short spell, the world) some twenty-five years earlier.

A big worry was removed for me on the eve of my first challenge for a professional championship. I had been scheduled to appear in the high court the morning after the fight. This was for the hearing to settle the long-running dispute over the piece of paper I had signed with another manager four years earlier. Terry knew it was weighing on my mind, and he instructed that the case be settled out of court. It meant I climbed into the Wembley ring in a perfect frame of mind. I was determined to do the best possible destruction job on Eklund to help pay Terry back for his faith in me.

As the Swede had come in so heavy for our fight I followed Terry's instructions to set a fast pace right from the first bell. There was a lot of the champion to hit and I scored frequently with stiff left jabs to the head that had him blinking. He seemed a little apprehensive every time I shaped to throw a right, but I was foxing him. I had no intention of letting my big bombs go until I knew I had made a proper opening.

Eklund threw few punches in this opening round, but managed to pierce my defence with a right to the body that made me remember to keep my elbows tucked in. My rat-a-tat-tat jabs brought blood trickling from his nose in the second round and this stirred him into his first big attack, but I was easily able to smother his punches with the tighter defence system that I had been perfecting during the long build-up to the fight.

Two big rights did get through to my head just before the bell, but they travelled too far to do any real damage, and I returned to my corner confident that I had his measure. He was beginning to puff because of all the weight he was carrying, and I knew that I had not even got properly warmed up yet.

'I think it's time to let him feel your right hand, Frank,' Terry said during the interval. 'But don't take any chances because he's

How many fingers am I holding up? The answer is eight and two seconds later Anders Eklund was counted out

dangerous with his right. Keep your chin tucked in and let your right go over his left lead.'

For the first minute of the round I gave Eklund no hint of my intentions. I kept the pattern as in the previous two rounds, jabbing to his head and throwing the occasional left hook. Then I let go with my first serious right, a long follow-through after a left lead. It caught Eklund high on the head and I knew it had hurt him. We tangled at close quarters and he hung on while his head cleared. The referee pulled us apart and I immediately threw two more quick rights and as they connected with the side of Eklund's head his long legs started to buckle. He had the sense to clutch hold of me and I banged in a left right combination that I felt would have floored him if he had not been so close to me and able to use me as a prop.

I couldn't wait for the fourth round to start. 'Now be careful,' Terry said, seeing the look of clear intent in my eyes. 'You've got him, but he is going to be trying a desperate right. Watch out for it.'

But I didn't give Eklund the chance. I almost ran to the centre of the ring and met him with a right over the top of his left lead that had him sagging at the knees. As his head came down towards me I jolted him with a right uppercut, and then followed with two very deliberate over-the-top rights that landed on the side of his massive jaw. He pitched forward to the canvas like a giant tree being felled. Eklund was sitting dazed in the centre of the ring with blood seeping from a cut over his left eye as Swiss referee Franz Marti counted him out.

I was the European champion and well on the way to my dream fight for the world heavyweight title. All the talk at the Press conference after my victory was of the world championship.

'How will you feel about fighting Michael Spinks for the IBF title?' I was asked.

'I'd fight a nine foot gorilla if the world championship was the prize,' I said.

'Did Eklund have you worried at all?'

'Yeah,' I said. 'I was frightened he was going to fall on me.' (I wasn't very proud of that cheap joke because Eklund had fought to the best of his ability, and I have a lot of time for him as a human being. He is a really nice man).

'How confident are you that you can win the world title?'

'Totally confident. I've always believed that one day I will be heavyweight champion of the world. When I lost to Bonecrusher Smith a lot of you gentlemen wrote me off. Fair enough. You are entitled to your opinions. But I knew I would come back and prove you all wrong. I hope you don't think I'm being flash. It's just that I have complete faith in myself, know what I mean?'

What are you going to do next?

I looked at Terry for guidance because I prefer him to answer those sort of questions. He smiled and shrugged.

'I'm going to take the dogs for a walk,' I said.

FIGHT No. 28
Opponent: **Larry Frazier (USA)**
Venue: **Royal Albert Hall**
Date: **4 December, 1985**

I was keyed up for a challenging battle against highly-regarded American Larry Alexander when, just three days before our fight, he failed the British Boxing Board of Control's strict medical check after a brain scan had revealed an irregularity. It was sad for Alexander, but provided further proof that medical supervision in British boxing is the best in the world.

They hastily brought in thirty-six-year-old Californian Larry Frazier as a

Larry Frazier takes it lying down after I had flattened him with two vicious body shots, but the victory gave me little satisfaction

substitute, and I got really nervous about this sudden change. I felt I was on a hiding to nothing against Frazier.

If I beat him, everybody would say: 'So what, he's an old man who should never have been in the ring with Bruno in the first place.' If I were to lose it might have destroyed my chances of a world title shot when I was within punching distance of the fight I have always dreamed about.

Terry had to be at his most persuasive to convince me that I had nothing to worry about. 'This is when you've got to prove to yourself what a great professional you've become,' he said. 'It's not the fight I

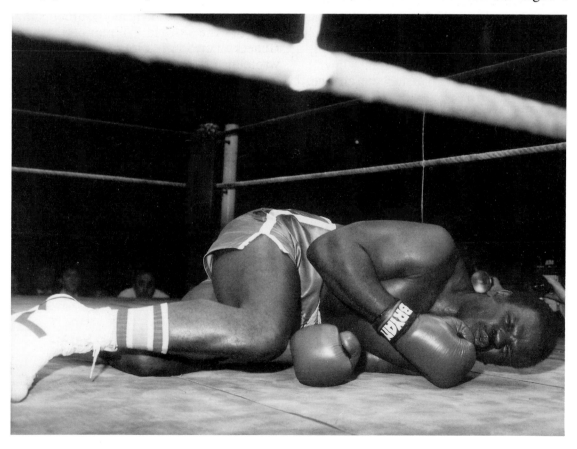

wanted for you, but you have got to climb into that ring with the sole intention of winning in the best style possible. I don't like you having to take this risk but we have no alternative. Look at it from the point of view that you still need all the experience you can get, and Frazier has been around long enough to be able to give you the ideal warm-up for your next fight which I can tell you in strictest confidence will almost certainly be an official eliminator for the world championship.'

Terry didn't have to say another word. I pushed all negative thoughts out of my head and suddenly looked on Frazier in a new light. Instead of seeing him as a veteran with little to offer I considered him to be the man standing between me and my dream. I was determined to knock him out of my path.

Frazier was yet another off that long production line of Americans who had been saved from a life of crime by the discipline and demands of boxing. He had served time in San Quentin, and the long gaps in his 14-year boxing career were due to brushes with the law. He confessed in pre-fight interviews that he was 'a womanizer and a gambler.' Frazier had stopped eighteen of his twenty-eight opponents inside the distance and said before our fight: 'I may not have the same speed and energy as ten years ago, but I still carry a knockout punch - as this guy Bruno is sure gonna find out.'

I was at my heaviest ever for the fight at a few ounces over 16 stone 3 pounds, but I was still having to give nine pounds to the heftily-built, 6 foot 4 inches tall American. His wide stomach looked an inviting target and I planted several short hooks into it during a first round in which Frazier provided little evidence that he carried the knockout power that he had been boasting about.

The thought that he could shatter my world title dreams with just one punch was uppermost in my mind as I came out for the second round, and I had made up my mind to try to get it over and done with at the first opportunity. I forced him back to the ropes with a series of left jabs and then buried two short, ripping left hooks into the side of his stomach.

If I had used a dagger the effect could not have been more dramatic. Frazier grunted as the punches sank in and he fell to the canvas and rolled over in agony. He was clasping his gloves to his stomach and groaning with pain as referee Roland Dakin counted him out.

I helped Frazier back to his corner and when he had recovered he told me: 'Man, all those things they say about you are true. You've got concrete in your gloves. Nobody's ever hit me like that before. I've worked with George Foreman, Joe Frazier, Ken Norton and Earnie Shavers - all the big punchers. And none of them hurt me downstairs the way you did tonight.'

It was flattering to hear him say it, but I wasn't really satisfied with my night's work. I would have been much happier if I had beaten a fighter of real quality. I was just relieved to have got Frazier out of the way without any scares. All my concentration was now on my *next* fight - an official eliminator for the world heavyweight championship.

It was lined up for my first fight of 1986, which my brother Michael had predicted long before would be my year of destiny.

FIGHT No. 29
Opponent: **Gerrie Coetzee (South Africa)**
Venue: **Wembley Arena**
Date: **4 March, 1986**

A white South African with a 'bionic' right hand was now all that stood between me and my dream of challenging for the heavyweight championship of the world, the greatest prize in sport.

I mention that he was white only because so many other people had made an issue of it. You will no doubt have noticed that throughout this first book of mine I have made little reference to the colour or creed of my opponents. I have never in my life been one for judging people by the shade of their skin. I take people as I find them.

The Anti-Apartheid Movement tried to put pressure on me not to go ahead with the fight with Gerrie Coetzee. Terry protected me as much as he could from the campaign aimed at me and the promotion, but the message got through that there were fanatical people who considered me some sort of a traitor for going through with the world title eliminator.

John Conteh, former world light-heavyweight champion and an old hero of mine, contacted me by letter putting the Anti-Apartheid Movement's case and asking me to consider pulling out of the fight rather than go into the ring with a white South African who had grown up under Apartheid laws.

I am not and never will be a political animal, but I have every sympathy with the case of the suppressed black people of South Africa. If I had thought not going ahead with the fight might have made any difference to their struggle for equality then I would have seriously considered refusing to fight.

But I knew in my heart that it would not have made the tiniest bit of difference. My act would have made front page headlines for a day or two and within a week would have been forgotten. 'Frank Who?' they would have said.

There would have been no winners if I had pulled out of the fight, and I would have been a big, big loser. I had fought my heart out to get this far in my career and there was no way I wanted to miss out on the chance of a lifetime. In effect, what the protesters would have achieved had they managed in their attempts to get the promotion cancelled was punish me because of the colour of *my* skin. Another point I took into consideration was that Coetzee himself was on record as being against Apartheid. He had dozens of black friends and his black sparring partner, Randy Stephens, was best man at his wedding. One more thing - I owed it to my family to go through with the contest. I am a professional sportsman and it is only through boxing that I can give Laura, Nicola and any other children God blesses us with security for life.

I shut the ban-the-fight argument out of my mind and got down to the serious business of training for the fight of my life. Coetzee was past the peak of his career, but he remained one of the most feared punchers in the game.

He was known as 'The Bionic Man' because the right fist with which he destroyed so many opponents had been operated on several times, and it was reported that the fist had been strengthened by the insertion of a steel pin. In thirty-five professional fights, Coetzee had been beaten just four times and only by top-flight opposition. John Tate had outpointed him over fifteen rounds in a WBA title fight in 1979, and big-hitting Mike Weaver had stopped him in the thirteenth round of a championship contest in 1980. In 1981 he

153

lost on points to Renaldo Snipes, and in a 1984 WBA title defence he had been knocked out by Greg Page during a controversial eighth round that had been allowed to run over time.

The greatest moment of his career so far had been a tenth round knockout victory over Mike Dokes that clinched the WBA version of the world heavyweight championship in 1983. He had also bombed out Leon Spinks and his countryman Kallie Knoetze, both in the first round, and he had held WBC heavyweight champion Pinklon Thomas to a draw. In his last fight before facing me he had scored an excellent points victory over a top American prospect, James 'Quick' Tillis.

There was criticism of him when he arrived in England accompanied by his wife and children. 'He seems to think he's over here on holiday,' was the sort of thing being said. But I believed Coetzee when he said that he felt more comfortable when his family was with him, and that it helped rather than hindered his concentration.

He seemed almost chillingly confident at one of the pre-fight Press conferences. 'Somebody's been lying to Frank,' he said. 'They've been filling his head with stories about me being involved in wars and that I'm not the fighter I was. He has been told that I am an easy short cut to the title. If the people telling him these things truly believe it then they have made the mistake of a lifetime. If he beats me then he will be the next world champ. But that's not going to happen.'

I made the boxing reporters chuckle when I said: 'I am 200 per cent confident that I will knock him out.' And I really honestly believed it. There was no way in this world that I was going to let him beat me.

At the weigh-in I scaled 16 stone 3 pounds, which was six and a quarter pounds lighter than the thirty-year-old South African, who was the same height as me. He repeated at the weigh-in that the people who had said he was 'over the top' were telling me lies. In actual fact, Terry had been telling me the exact opposite. 'You've got to treat him with great respect,' he said. 'He is second only to Earnie Shavers as the biggest puncher of the last fifteen years.'

Coetzee tried the old Ali trick of staring me down as we got our last-minute instructions from the referee in the centre of the ring, but I held his stare until he dropped his gaze. I had won the eyeball-to-eyeball confrontation. Now it was time for the real stuff.

In our pre-fight planning, Terry, Jimmy Tibbs, Frank Black and I had decided that I should try to get a big punch in as early as possible to test Coetzee's chin and his confidence. I would usually have gone out jabbing for the first couple of minutes before throwing any 'nuclear' punches, but I wanted Coetzee to know as quickly as possible that I carried a dig to match his famous 'bionic' right. While doing our homework on him we noticed that every time he threw a left jab his head came up. 'The moment he jabs,' said Terry, 'he is wide open to a right counter. So watch for the opening.'

In the opening minute I backed him up to the ropes with a succession of left leads and then, just as he jabbed with his left, his head came up and I launched my right with a full follow-through of my right shoulder. The knuckle part of my glove connected with his left cheekbone, and Coetzee sat down as if somebody had suddenly pulled a chair from under him. He was up quickly at three, and as he stood taking the mandatory eight count blood started to run down from a cut where my punch had landed. I could see by the glazed look in his eyes that I had hurt him more than he was letting on. I decided there and then to go all out for a quick finish.

That genius of a photographer Eamonn McCabe captures the final moments of my world title eliminator against Gerrie Coetzee. There goes the right...and there goes Coetzee...through the ropes and out to the world

As Canadian referee Guy Jutras waved me back into the fight I met Coetzee with full-power left jabs. He tried to grab my arms and pull me to him, but I pushed him off and drove him back across the ring towards his own corner. I was so keen to get to him while he was still dazed that I tried too hard and missed with two over-the-top rights. Coetzee retreated to the far side of the ring and shaped as if he was about to try his first attack of the fight, but before he could let his punches go I connected with as hard a right cross as I had ever thrown. The punch hit him on the side of the jaw and snapped his head sideways.

He collapsed back across the bottom rope and the force of my punch was so great that half his huge body was hanging over the apron, pinning an unfortunate cameraman to his seat. It was obvious that the fight was over for the unconscious Coetzee. The referee started to count but the noise of the crowd was so great that I couldn't hear it. And poor Coetzee certainly couldn't because he was out to the world. The referee waved his arms to signal that it was all over, and the MC announced: 'After one minute fifty seconds of the first round the referee has stopped the contest.' Some of the newspapers reported that it was a knockout, but Mr Jutras told me: 'I didn't complete the count, Frank, because I was worried for Gerrie's safety. Sorry to rob you of a k.o. in the record book, but I know you'll understand.'

We were concerned about Coetzee for several minutes, but he then recovered sufficiently to return to his corner. Later in his dressing-room he was sporting enough to tell me: 'Frank, I have been fighting for more than twenty years. Nobody has ever done to me what you did tonight. You were magnificent, and I'm going to tell everybody that you will be the next world champion. Good luck to you. You've got a great career to look forward to. This is only the beginning.'

And this was the man they wanted to ban. He didn't see me as black Frank Bruno. He saw me as Frank Bruno, human being. And I saw him as Gerrie Coetzee, human being and great sportsman.

Back in my dressing-room it was sheer bedlam. Eamonn Andrews and *This Is Your Life* producer Malcolm Morris pushed their way into the crowded room to congratulate me and Terry made Eamonn give that famous laugh of his when he called out: 'Not now Eamonn...'

I apparently talked non-stop to the Press for so long that one reporter turned to Terry and said: 'I've filled five pages of my notebook and I haven't had to ask a question yet...'

'How does it feel, Frank, to know that your next fight will be for the heavyweight championship of the world?'

'I don't want to seem flash but I've always known I would get this far in my career. And you haven't seen the best of me yet. I know I can be a lot better.'

'Did you think you could beat Coetzee so quickly?'

'You can't plan to knock out a fighter of his class in the first round. I wanted to get a big punch in early just so that he would respect me. You saw what happened. The first big right I landed, down he went. That's when I knew I could get it over quickly.'

'Did you honestly think you would get this far after that knockout defeat by Bonecrusher Smith here in this same arena less than two years ago?'

'I've never had any doubts. I'm lucky to have a great manager in Terry Lawless and two of the best trainers in Jimmy Tibbs and Frank Black. They helped me get over that defeat and learn from the mistakes that I made. Mind you, that defeat really hurt. It was like your wife leaving you when you loved her. It really was as bad as that.

'Old Bonecrusher. He was some guy. I really liked him, you know. And how about that name! Imagine telling your daughter that you are going off to fight. And she says: 'Who are you fighting, Daddy?' And you say: 'A man called Bonecrusher.' And she says: 'B-b-b-Bonecrusher! Please don't go, Daddy. Please don't fight the Bonecrusher.'

(I got a big laugh from the Press boys with that story)

'How did you feel when Coetzee tried to outstare you just before the first bell?'

'There was no way I was going to look away. He could have brought his wife and kids into the ring with him, plus a big baboon and a sledgehammer and I would still have beaten him. That's how confident I felt. A lot of you have been saying that I've been fighting stiffs and bums. Well nobody can say Gerrie Coetzee isn't a top quality fighter. He was the number one contender and a former champion. Now I'm the number one contender and, please God, the future champion. I'm not saying I'm the best heavyweight in the world. I can't do the sweet-as-lollipop shuffles like Ali used to. But there's nobody fitter and stronger than me. And nobody punches harder than me. Ask Gerrie Coetzee.'

Terry Lawless then made a throwaway comment: 'The way you're talking, Frank, you could fill a book.'

I looked at him and said: 'That's a good idea, Tel. We can call it *Know What I Mean?* **Know what I mean?'**

The final word: 'Fanks very much, 'Arry...know what I mean?'

For the Record

THE BRUNO FILE

Born Hammersmith General Hospital, 16 November 1961.
Weight at birth: nine pounds. **Star Sign:** Scorpio.
Mother Lynette, a district nurse. **Father** Robert, died 1975.
Elder brothers Michael and Eddie. **Elder sisters** Faye, Angela and Joanne.
Schools: Swaffield Primary, Wandsworth, and Oak Hall Boarding School, Sussex.
Represented Sussex Schools at football and athletics. He was head boy in his final year at Oak Hall. Started boxing at the age of nine with the Wandsworth Boys Club. Won an NABC title on a walk-over. Boxed three times as a junior. All his contests were against Gary Hill. Each bout went the distance, with Bruno winning two and Hill one.
Amateur career: 21 contests, 20 victories (avenged his only defeat by Irish international Joe Christle). Boxed for the Sir Philip Game Amateur Boxing Club, 1977-1980. In his final season as an amateur he represented Young England, and won the London ABA and national ABA heavyweight titles. At eighteen, he was the youngest ever ABA heavyweight champion.
Professional from 1982 following an operation in Bogota to correct short-sightedness in his right eye.
Managed by Terry Lawless. Trainers Jimmy Tibbs and Frank Black. Gymnasium: The Royal Oak, Barking Road, Canning Town, London.
Ring record (to July, 1986): 29 fights, 28 victories. His only defeat was by James 'Bonecrusher' Smith, who won on a 10th round knockout at Wembley on May 13 1984. It was Bruno's 22nd contest. Total rounds as a professional: 85. Has scored thirteen clean knockouts. European champion 1985-86 (relinquished it to concentrate on his world championship challenge).
Tale of the Tape: Height 6ft. 3in.; weight 16st. 3lbs.; reach 82in.; boots 12in.; calf 16in.; thigh 24in.; biceps 16in.; neck 18in.; chest 43in. (47in. expanded); fist 14in; forearm 14in.; wrist 9in.; waist 33in.; ankle 10in.;
Personal: Lives with girlfriend Laura in a modern town house in Essex, a 25-minute drive from the Royal Oak Gymnasium. They have a three-year-old daughter, Nicola, and expect a second child in September. **Personal dislikes:** Reporters invading my privacy or anybody interrupting my training routine.
Boyhood heroes: Muhammad Ali and John Conteh (boxing); Peter Osgood (football); Gary Sobers and Michael Holding (cricket).
Hobbies: Swimming, roller skating, chess, listening to jazz-funk, soul and reggae, driving (has a Ford Granada Ghia). Eating. Buying good clothes. Watching old-time boxers on video (his favourite is Joe Louis).
Favourite singers: Marvin Gaye, Bob Marley, Bruce Springsteen and Stevie Wonder; **Favourite television programmes:** EastEnders and Only Fools and Horses. **Favourite actors:** Clint Eastwood and James Cagney; **Favourite actresses:** Joan Collins and Anita Dobson; **Favourite comedians:** Lenny Henry and Norman Wisdom.
Ambition: 'One and one only - to win the heavyweight championship of the world, know what I mean?'

Bruno's Path to a World Title Fight

17. 3.82	Lupe Guerra (Mexico)	w.ko.1	Royal Albert Hall
30. 3.82	Harvey Steichen (USA)	w.rsf.2	Wembley Arena
20. 4.82	Tom Stevenson (USA)	w.ko.1	Royal Albert Hall
4. 5.82	Ron Gibbs (USA)	w.rsf.4	Wembley Arena
1. 6.82	Tony Moore (GB)	w.rsf.2	Royal Albert Hall
14. 9.82	George Scott (GB)	w.rsf.1	Wembley Arena
23.10.82	Ali Lukusa (Zaire)	w.ko.2	West Berlin
9.11.82	Rudi Gauwe (Belgium)	w.ko.2	Royal Albert Hall
23.11.82	George Butzbach (W. Germany)	w.ret.1	Wembley Arena
7.12.82	Gilberto Acuna (Puerto Rica)	w.rsf.1	Royal Albert Hall
18. 1.83	Stewart Lithgo (GB)	w.ret.4	Royal Albert Hall
8. 2.83	Peter Mulendwa (Uganda)	w.ko.3	Royal Albert Hall
1. 3.83	Winston Allen (GB)	w.rsf.2	Royal Albert Hall
5. 4.83	Eddie Neilson (GB)	w.rsf.3	Royal Albert Hall
3. 5.83	Scott LeDoux (USA)	w.rsf.3	Wembley Arena
31. 5.83	Barry Funches (USA)	w.rsf.5	Royal Albert Hall
9. 7.83	Mike Jameson (USA)	w.ko.2	Chicago
27. 9.83	Bill Sharkey (USA)	w.ko.1	Wembley Arena
11.10.83	Floyd Cummings (USA)	w.rsf.7	Royal Albert Hall
6.12.83	Walter Santemore (USA)	w.ko.4	Royal Albert Hall
13. 3.84	Juan Figueroa (Argentina)	w.ko.1	Wembley Arena
13. 5.84	James 'Bonecrusher' Smith (USA)	l.ko.10	Wembley Arena
25. 9.84	Ken Lakusta (Canada)	w.ko.2	Wembley Arena
	(Commonwealth championship eliminator)		
6.11.84	Jeff Jordan (USA)	w.rsf.3	Royal Albert Hall
27.11.84	Phil Brown (USA)	w.pts.10	Wembley Arena
26. 3.85	Lucien Rodriguez (France)	w.rsf.1	Wembley Arena
1.10.85	Anders Eklund (Sweden)	w.ko.4	Wembley Arena
	(European heavyweight championship)		
4.12.85	Larry Frazier (USA)	w.ko.2	Royal Albert Hall
4. 3.86	Gerrie Coetzee (South Africa)	w.rsf.1	Wembley Arena
	(WBA world heavyweight championship, final eliminator)		